848.91208   70642
St6g

DATE DUE			

GAYLORD M-2   PRINTED IN U.S.A.

Crosscurrents/MODERN CRITIQUES

Crosscurrents/MODERN CRITIQUES

Harry T. Moore, *General Editor*

Gide's Eagles

Ben Stoltzfus

WITH A PREFACE BY
Harry T. Moore

SOUTHERN ILLINOIS UNIVERSITY PRESS
Carbondale and Edwardsville

FEFFER & SIMONS, INC.
London and Amsterdam

To Jan, Celia, and Andrew

Preface

This book appears just a century after André Gide's birth in 1869. Gide had a long life; he did not die until 1951. Usually an author's reputation sinks in the years after his death, but Gide's has not, and interest in him remains strong. The bibliography in the present book shows how many books about him have appeared in recent years.

Gide had attracted the attention of the literary world from the beginning, although his first book, Les Cahiers d'André Walter (1891), was published anonymously. It consisted of two fictional notebooks by a young man doomed to meet an early death. This "novel" has often been compared to Goethe's Leiden des jungen Werthers, and while it did not have the world-wide success of Werther, André Walter was nevertheless well received, and was praised by Mallarmé and Maeterlinck. In later years, long after the authorship had been acknowledged, Gide said that the fervently romantic tone of this early book "exasperated" him. But many characteristics of his later work are evident in André Walter, and even its plot bears a certain resemblance to some of the later books.

In the preceding paragraph I was careful not to use the word novel without quotation marks. Gide did not apply this term even to such standard-type works of fiction as Les Caves du Vatican (1914), a comedy (which includes a murder) about a gang of crooks who pretend that the Pope has been abducted and who raise money ostensibly to rescue him and to do away with the imposter who has supplanted him. Gide called this and various other of his fictional works soties, taking the word from that of a type of medieval satirical farce; and some of his writings he merely called récits, or narratives. But he spoke of Les Faux-Monnayeurs (1926), another story built around an author's notebook, as a novel.

Most of Gide's work, indeed, was fictional, often an elaboration of mythological themes. He became a great man of belles-lettres, but his eminence was a lonely one. In 1937, when he first met Claude Mauriac, he told the young man that he had gone twice to the films that day because of loneliness.

That loneliness, however, that necessary loneliness, had produced the books about which so many others have been written. And now we have this new one by Professor Ben F. Stoltzfus of the University of California at Riverside. He provides a fresh reading of André Gide, based on that author's use of the eagle as a symbol of various kinds—not, as Mr. Stoltzfus carefully points out, in the manner of the Symbolist poets whom Gide knew in his youth.

Professor Stoltzfus has written an earlier volume in this Crosscurrents series, Alain Robbe-Grillet and the New French Novel (1964). He has also had a book published in Paris, Georges Chennevière et l'unanimisme (Menard, 1965). In 1967 Viking Press of New York published Mr. Stoltzfus' novel, The Eye of the Needle. He brings a varied and valuable experience of studying and writing to his examination of Gide.

HARRY T. MOORE

Southern Illinois University
September 11, 1968

Contents

Introduction

I owe thanks in general to colleagues and students whose intelligence, judgment, and sensibility have added so much to my own evaluation of André Gide's work. Specifically I wish to thank Professors Jean-Pierre Barricelli, William Mead, Herbert Linderberger, and Naomi Lebowitz for their thoughtful comments and wise suggestions in editing the manuscript. I am grateful to the graduate students in my Gide seminar for the incisiveness of their reactions in listening to the early chapters of the book.

A Fulbright-Hays Research Grant to Paris expedited the reading of the almost inexhaustible supply of secondary material on Gide. For this I am indebted to the United States Government. A liberal research grant from the University of California, as well as from its Institute in the Humanities, enabled me to finish this study sooner than I could have otherwise. For this I am also grateful.

The dust jacket reprint of André Gide is there by the permission and kindness of Mrs. Theodore Steinert. The original is a sanguine by William Rothenstein. Chapter 8, *Saul, Oedipus, and God,* first appeared in modified form in the *French Review.* I wish to thank the editor for permission to include it here.

As for the quotations from Gide's work I am indebted to my wife, Elizabeth, for the faithful, graceful, and nuanced way in which she has Englished the French. We did our own translations (though we gratefully acknowledge the help of Justin O'Brien's excellent translation of Gide's *Journals*) because I was working from the French text and wanted to preserve the exact flavor of my commentary.

Permission to quote from Gide's works has been granted by the Librairie Gallimard and, for *L'Immoraliste*, by the Mercure de France. All references to Gallimard editions are from the following books: the three-volume Pléiade edition of *Journal 1889–1939* (Paris, 1948), *Journal 1939–1948* (Paris, 1954), and *Romans, récits et soties* (Paris, 1958); the one-volume edition of Gide's *Théâtre* (1942); the *Correspondance Paul Claudel et André Gide, 1899–1926* (Paris, 1949); and the *Correspondance Francis Jammes et André Gide, 1893–1938* (Paris, 1948).

Permission to use my own English translations has been authorized by all American and British publishers except Random House. I hereby acknowledge Random House's generous insistence that I use John Russell's translation for the Claudel-Gide Correspondence. The other permissions, gratefully acknowledged, have been granted by the following publishers who own American and British rights to the following books: Cassell and Company, Ltd.: *The Immoralist, The Pastoral Symphony, The School for Wives, Vatican Cellars*; Alfred A. Knopf, Inc.: *Fruits of the Earth, The Immoralist, The Journals of André Gide, 1889–1949, New Fruits of the Earth, The Pastoral Symphony, The School for Wives, Theseus, The Vatican Swindle*; New Directions: *Dostoevsky*; Secker and Warburg, Ltd.: *The Correspondence between Paul Claudel and André Gide, Dostoevsky, Fruits of the Earth, The Journals of André Gide, 1889–1949, New Fruits of the Earth, Return of the Prodigal, Theseus*; Utah State University: *The Return of the Prodigal Son*.

Some readers will undoubtedly wish I had spent more time evaluating Gide criticism. This is not that kind of book. To have done so would have doubled its size and weakened the handling of my metaphor, the *eagle*, which, as it is, flies back and forth between such standard themes as the Gidean "dialogue," authenticity, and the counterfeit. The eagle is, nevertheless, an original bird. Still, it seems to me appropriate to thank all Gide scholars and critics whose opinions I have borrowed, either consciously or inadvertently, who do not appear in footnotes.

For convenience, in handling the Gidean "dialogue," I have adopted Erich Fromm's ethical *structure* of the humanistic and authoritarian conscience as expounded in his early work, particularly *Man for Himself,* because Gide's own value system functions so well within this dialectic. Fromm's later work does not seem as relevant nor have I made any attempt, using Jean Delay's two volumes, entitled *La Jeunesse d'André Gide,* as a point of departure, to explore the full range of possible comparisons between Gide, Fromm, modern psychology, sociology, and psychiatry. That is a topic for an entirely new and different study.

Nor have I treated Gide's works chronologically because Gide, himself, affirmed that the ideas from which all of them crystallized had already been conceived, almost simultaneously, sometime in the 1890's. The reader will, nevertheless, note some kind of progression from internalized *eagles* to Church *eagles* to social *eagles* —an evolution which corresponds, roughly, to the direction and emphasis of Gide's art and thought as it evolved from the early 1890's to the time of his death in 1951.

Chapter 1, *Prometheus,* stresses Gide's wish to break the chains of man's moral conformity and subservience to the gods. Chapter 2, *The Symbolist Eagle,* analyzes several works generally ascribed to Gide's "symbolist" period, describes the manner in which Gide cultivated the "fin de siècle" aestheticism emanating from Mallarmé's "Tuesdays," and defines Gide's emancipation from it. Chapter 3, *The Immoral Gate,* a study of *L'Immoraliste* (1902) and *La Porte étroite* (1909), isolates and reveals two of the most clearly defined species of internal eagle which thrive on "extremes" of human behavior. Chapter 4, *The Pastoral Symphony* (1919), while demonstrating the pitfalls of Protestant "conscience," sketches the outline of the Protestant-Catholic "dialogue" which will be fully explored in the next two chapters. Chapter 5, *The Protestant Eagle*, contrasts André Walter's asceticism with the fulfilled, unabashed lyricism of *Les Nourritures terrestres*. Gide plucks one Protestant eagle in 1897, then, deliberately, revives a Phoenix from the ashes of a Puritan morality, long discarded, in order to observe and record in *Numquid et tu . . . ?* and in his 1916–18 *Journal* the psychosomatic lacerations of claws and beak. This chapter and the next will, I believe, provide confirmed Gideans with some interesting conclusions and new juxtapositions.

Chapter 6, *The Catholic Dialogue*, describes Gide's moral, aesthetic, and epistolary confrontation with Catholicism. I have deliberately combined a discussion of *Le Retour de l'enfant prodigue* (1907), *Les Caves du Vatican* (1914), Gide's correspondence and "dialogue" with Paul Claudel, Francis Jammes, Charles Du Bos, and Henri Massis with Gide's particular synthesis of Nietzsche and Dostoevsky because, it seemed to me, only in this way could I give full range to the complexity of Gide's moral stance in opposition to the Vatican's condemnation of his works.

Chapter 7, *Counterfeiters*, moves from Catholic eagles to other social species with a discussion of *Les Faux-Monnayeurs* (1926) and to an authoritarian kind of family eagle with an analysis of *L'Ecole des femmes* (1929). Chapter 8, *Saul, Oedipus, and God*, explores two of Gide's favorite inspirational sources, Christianity and Greek mythology, and demonstrates the moral distance Oedipus' "freedom" has traveled (1931) since Saul's abortive rebellion against God (1903). Oedipus and Theseus are Gide's two supreme moral heroes in the sense that they have the wisdom, the luck, and the tenacity to discard or avoid eagles. Their "liberation" affirms the inviolate dignity of man.

Finally, in Chapter 9, Theseus' escape from the labyrinth sums up the moral and aesthetic odyssey of Gide's characters as they struggle with, succumb to, or free themselves from the tyrannical clutches of eagles which would deny their true human potential. Varied as Gide's fiction is, it is self-contained, even coherent, and from *Les Cahiers d'André Walter* (1891) to *Thésée* (1946) we can chart Gide's labyrinth of values. Aesthetically he described bondage, self-deception, spiritual blindness, and submission to authority, but morally Gide's thread leads us toward insight, creativity, and freedom. Perhaps the ultimate freedom of subservience to a cause.

BEN STOLTZFUS

17 January 1967
University of California
Riverside

Gide's Eagles

I was like Prometheus astonished that one could live with-out an eagle and without being devoured by it.

Si le grain ne meurt

1

Prometheus

One day, high in the Caucasus, Prometheus discovers that his chains, tenons, straitjackets, parapets, and other scruples are ankylosing him. In order to change position, he lifts his left side, stretches his right hand and, between four and five o'clock in the Fall, walks along the boulevard leading from the Madeleine to the Opéra. He sits down at a café, orders a beer, and asks the waiter where everybody is going.[1]

In *Le Promethée mal enchaîné* (1899) Gide is asserting, in a less doctrinaire manner than Sartre does in *Les Mouches* (1943), that man is not dependent on the gods. Like Orestes flaunting his freedom in Jupiter's face and subsequently liberating Argos from a scourge of flies (Argos's remorse for having condoned Agamemnon's murder), Prometheus would also free man of his subservience to eagles. Whereas the legendary Prometheus was freed by Hercules, Gide's Prometheus, like Sartre's Orestes, need only stretch to break his chains. In both the old and the new versions the eagle is presumed to be an affliction, but in Gide's, the bird will feed only when summoned. Otherwise he remains as hungry and scrawny as a vulture. Nevertheless, Prometheus believes that the eagle is good for him. He even gives a sparkling lecture with fireworks in which he praises its usefulness. But when he discovers that Damocles died for his eagle and that Zeus, the banker, has none because he is the one who gives them, Prometheus slaughters his feathered tormentor and eats him. After the meal Gide informs us that he has written the story with an eagle quill.

Gide's eagle or the eagles of his fictional characters are direct descendants of the bird that once fed on Prometheus. The eagle is an internal or external obstacle which frustrates the physical, moral, and intellectual growth of man. An internal eagle is the voice of conscience, passion, sensuality, or asceticism which is responsible for the "bad faith" Sartre, in turn, alludes to so frequently. An external eagle may be a person, the family, the Church, society, or the State which, in the name of some "higher authority" tries to bind man with chains of moral conformity.

Gide's aviculture exposes the flaws of internalized as well as the dangers of externalized dogma. His fiction, his *Journal*, and his correspondence set up a dialogue of opposites which Gide's intellect balances like a tightrope act. He moves dexterously from one extreme to the other but almost always, it seems, with a sense of detached irony. He is forever cultivating the seed (*Si le grain ne meurt*) of human potential which can be destroyed if absolutism, social duplicity, and ignorance combine with inordinate and "fatalistic" weight to snuff it out.

If we can imagine a Gide-Prometheus fattening the eagles of his artistic imagination, then we can read his books as a description of the false roads men have traveled in search of themselves. Each of these roads is one he himself might have taken had it not been for the fact that, in writing a particular book, he exposes the excesses of a character and thereby simultaneously purges himself of similar obsessions. Gide's works are signposts on the way toward a new kind of "paradise." From Narcissus contemplating his image in the river to Theseus' interview with Oedipus, Gide's books point the way. Each one of them is a moral voyage.

Urien's voyage leads him to the stagnant waters of the Polar Sea. The prophet prince in *El Hadj* leads his people to the equally stagnant marshes of the desert. *Paludes* describes the stagnation of a certain kind of hermetic symbolism. The prodigal son, because of an inherent flaw in his makeup, takes the wrong road. So do Saul, Alissa, Michel, the Pastor, Vincent, Robert, and as many others.

Gide's work is indeed, as Charles Du Bos observed, a labyrinth of false exits, a maze which leads certain characters to self-destruction. The Minotaur is within them and, like the eagle, either imprisons or devours its victims. It is therefore appropriate, using the labyrinth as metaphor, that Gide should have used Theseus as his last fictional character. If we are all modern Theseuses, wandering through the labyrinth of a gratuitous world, that is, if progress is a snare and there is no "raison d'être," except perhaps the process of living itself, then Gide's work is a thread which, though it may not lead back to Ariadne, at least clearly shows where the eagles and false exits are located.[2]

With the publication of *Les Nouvelles nourritures* in 1935 Gide defined the progress of which he disapproved as well as the particular human kind of progress he felt was viable.

> I too, to be sure, have been able to smile or laugh with Flaubert at the idol of Progress; but it is because progress was presented to us as a ridiculous deity. Progress of commerce and industry; of the arts especially, what folly! Progress of knowledge, yes, certainly. But what really matters to me is the progress of Mankind.[3]

The progress Gide envisions for man will be one toward moral and psychic equilibrium—a progress away from eagles.

Yet, in *Le Prométhée mal enchaîné*, Damocles dies because he "trod the middle road—without realizing that the extremes touch each other" (p. 308). Gide, in contrast to Damocles, cultivates the extremes. He, the artist, is the point of contact for contradictory eagles. In *La Porte étroite* Alissa will listen to the voice of an ascetic conscience which will destroy her. Her eagle is heroic while Michel (the protagonist of *L'Immoraliste*), who sacrifices his wife, Marceline, listens to the voice of a passionate eagle which atrophies his sense of moral responsibility to others. Gide used these extremes, these two eagles, alternately, because, to have adopted the "juste milieu," as expressed in the final serenity of his *Thésée* would have implied the early death of his art. Gide deliberately fattened the birds of his two "consciences" for the sake of moral and psychological verisimilitude.

While Gide's two "consciences" are in constant artistic dialogue, his greatest eagle, which he seems to have spent half his life exorcising, was subservience to and escape from authority. That is the point at which the "two extremes," like night and day, meet. Dawn is, therefore, a marvelous time for embarking on new voyages and it is relevant, perhaps, that Urien's departure, in *Le Voyage d'Urien*, takes place at that time.

The imaginary voyages in Gide's fiction will lead him out of the prison of moral imperatives. For him, the artist, the best escape is, like Prometheus, to use the eagle of his Protestant conscience, fatten it on guilt, fly out of the cell of religious authoritarianism and then, once liberated, slaughter the offending bird and transform the experience into a work of art.

In spite of Gide's vision of authority as a great winged beast he, like Baudelaire, had one eagle which postulated God (Alissa in *La Porte étroite*) and another which claimed Satan (Michel in *L'Immoraliste*). While Gide frequently interchanged the two for the delectation of his admirers or the anger of his critics, he capitalized on the possibilities for dramatic dialogue between the two and sought repeatedly to focus attention on the duality of his religious, cultural, biological, and geographical backgrounds. Two favorite sources from which he drew inspiration, as *Le Prométhée mal enchaîné* suggests, were the Bible and Greek mythology. Gide used these sources separately, as in *Philoctète* (Greek) or *Saül* (Old Testament) or fused them, as in *Le Voyage d'Urien* and *Oedipe*. He emphasized this same duality in Western culture, particularly in France, and never was he more insistent on being French than when World War II threatened to extinguish the European blend of the Judeo-Christian and Greco-Roman tradition.

This very insistence suggests that Gide considered him-

self a product and at the same time a synthesis of North-
ern and Southern France, of Protestantism and Catholicism, of the "langue d'oïl" and of the "langue d'oc." In
the ethical realm his work embodies the opposition of
authoritarian and permissive values. In Gide's books eagles are fattened whenever a character suppresses human
values and replaces them with a doctrinaire subservience
to authoritarian beliefs. Since in Gide's works eagles do
not have man's best interest at heart, they should be killed
or, if need be, exploited, but never tolerated for long.
"The eagle in any case devours us, vice or virtue, duty or
passion," says Prometheus (p. 327).

Polarized by eagles, Gide's fiction, his plays, his essays,
his *Journal*, and his correspondence are one enormous
aesthetic and moral dialogue. There is no facet of it which
he does not use or bend to his needs. The most persistent
voices stress the dialogue of opposites: the permissive
versus the arbitrary, the free versus the authoritarian, the
spontaneous versus the peremptory. Characters like André
Walter and Alissa are the victims of the arbitrary, the
authoritarian, and the doctrinaire while Nathanaël, Lafcadio, and Bernard are permissive, free, and spontaneous.

Conscience, as one of several eagles, alternately whis-
pers words of duty, virtue, sin, guilt, or remorse. Conscience, in fact, is a winged voice which speaks in the
name of God, church, or family, so that if we have obeyed
it, we feel "good," whereas, if we have disobeyed it, we
feel guilty or "bad." One of the most pertinent examples
of conscience as a "voice" comes to us from the life of
Saint Francis of Assisi. Charles Berthond Hase writes that
St. Francis is said to have declared upon his deathbed that
he had sinned against the body by subjecting it to unusual
privations. At prayer one night he allegedly heard a voice
saying: "Francis, there is no sinner in the world whom if
he be converted, God will not pardon; but he who kills
himself by hard penances will find no mercy in eternity." [4]
It is said that St. Francis attributed this voice to the devil.

The ascetic fervor of Saint Francis, or Saint Alexis, or
Saint Leger who renounced the world in order to live in

privation, sustains itself in the belief that the mortification of the flesh on earth must necessarily multiply the future rewards in heaven. But let us suppose for a moment, as seems to have been the case with Saint Francis and the voice he heard, that the body rebels against the tyranny of such counsel. Traditionally, such rebellion, and the voices which accompany it, has been blamed on the devil. It need not surprise us, therefore, that Saint Francis should accuse the devil of subverting his pious intentions. Within the "spirit is good" versus the "flesh is evil" dichotomy, would it not be consistent with such premises to suspect any voice that wished to curry favor with the flesh? If, however, we no longer suspect the body and if, as modern medicine tells us, we react psychosomatically to a total situation, is it not possible that the voice Saint Francis heard, instead of being the devil's was the desperate plea of life asking not to be killed?

Should we not argue that privations which prematurely destroy the body are a violation of life as well as the natural processes of the living and that the voice Saint Francis heard was not the devil, but the voice of self-preservation? If we accept this argument, then we realize that the voices of conscience are not only contradictory but also reversible and, depending upon our premises, can either be the voice of the devil or the voice of God.

It is with such a dichotomy in mind that Erich Fromm, for instance, defines what he calls the authoritarian and the humanistic conscience. The *authoritarian conscience* is "the voice of an internalized external authority, the parents, the state, or whoever the authorities in a culture happen to be." [5] The *humanistic conscience*, in contrast to the authoritarian, is not the internalized voice of an authority we might be eager to please and afraid of displeasing, but an inner voice, independent of external sanctions and rewards.[6] The humanistic conscience is the voice of an inner self which prompts man to live productively, fully, and harmoniously in the direction of the self's true potential. It guards the integrity of the self and protects it from authoritarian voices which might be doing violence to it.

The voice Saint Francis heard, therefore, seems to be a dramatic confrontation of the authoritarian and the humanistic consciences.

Gide's fictional characters, good Protestants that most of them are, wrestle with similar consciences—voices which Gide transforms into eagles, angels, or devils, depending upon the nature of the particular confrontation. Gide, however, is suspicious of "conscience" and the three books which analyze the problem of inner voices in greatest detail, *L'Immoraliste*, *La Porte étroite*, and *La Symphonie pastorale*, reveal the masks which self-interest, in keeping with La Rochefoucauld's maxims, parades under the guise of "conscience."

Nevertheless, in spite of the fact that Gide suspects "conscience," both he and Fromm are in search of man's pure uncontaminated self. Fromm postulated as a precondition for the discovery of "authenticity" that man discard the false voices of conscience, which he calls authoritarian, so that the real voice of conscience, which he calls humanistic, may be heard. This means that social convention, parental convention, religious doctrine, in other words, all predetermined moral systems, must be cast off or seriously questioned before the individual can know whether his behavior is the result of imposed values or whether it corresponds to the actual needs of an uncontaminated self. The phenomenon of repression which psychiatrists so emphatically stress and which Norman O. Brown in his book *Life Against Death* says is the source of man's historical neurosis, occurs presumably whenever the needs of the authentic self are thwarted.

The civilizing force of Christianity, for instance, and the authoritarian "thou shalt nots" of the Ten Commandments, by reinforcing law and order, may have made our environment a safer place in which to live. But if Nietzsche is right, Christianity has achieved this victory at the expense of everything that is "noble" and vital in man. Nietzsche's diatribe against Christianity as an ethic which has thwarted the spontaneity and vigor of Western man is, in part, a reaction against an ethical system which, he claims, has forced man to live inauthentically. If, historically speaking, the only way to make man behave was to threaten him with punishment in hell or with rewards in heaven, then Christianity had to invent a force, God, which would insure that the just were rewarded and the evil ones chastised. God, therefore, as a source of "civilizing" morality was an external authority imposing outside sanctions on man.

Nietzsche's description of this historical process stresses the conflict between the nobility and the masses. His polemic is, as he admits, deliberately one-sided and controversial, particularly his analysis of the role the Jews played in the war of nonresistance between Judea and Rome and, by extension, against the nobility of all nations. For Nietzsche nobility alone is spontaneous, aggressive, warlike, hostile, and natural. Europe's masses, therefore, in the course of the past two thousand years, have found solace in the belief that in heaven they would be first and the nobles, that is the rich, would be last. (Is it not easier for a camel to go through the eye of a needle than for a rich man to enter into the kingdom of God?) One dimension of Christianity (which in no way does justice to other vital elements in it) has taught submission (the meek shall inherit the kingdom of God), passivity, and the belief that suffering, abstinence, and the absence of joy on earth will be rewarded in heaven. Suffering and renunciation therefore become a means to an end, and the devout Christian who believes in these means or who rationalizes them because he cannot or will not do anything to improve his lot on earth no doubt finds comfort in the belief that the rich, or the wicked, or the wayward will receive their just deserts. The righteous man therefore will strive to enter heaven via the "strait gate."

This aspect of Christianity has taught man to suppress and repress (either out of necessity or for the higher ideal —the latter being Alissa's goal in *La Porte étroite*) immediate joys and satisfactions for the sake of the life everlasting. Certain human drives, either basic or acquired, will then be inhibited whenever they come in conflict with an ethical code which preaches austerity, asceticism, and the postponement of joy. For those who believe in God's divine justice such a renunciation is acceptable and, from all evidence, even a source of satisfaction. Nevertheless, a majority of men seem incapable of such "heroism."

One of the reasons men seem incapable of such heroism is that it negates living. The other reason, advanced by Albert Camus, is that our present existence is the only guarantee of life we have and therefore must be lived. There is an unequivocal opposition here between those who live for the present and those who would live for the future. Moreover, the persistence of the Tristan and the Don Juan myths in Western literature seems to confirm this inherent conflict between two mutually exclusive value systems. Tristan believes in a resurrection and in the transfiguration of love in death whereas Don Juan, obsessed by time and flux believes only in an immediate and ephemeral love. Tristan postpones loving Isolde because he believes this delay necessary for the survival of their love after death, while Don Juan, who believes in no afterlife, and is hyperconscious of death as tragedy, loves frenetically in an attempt to fill the void of a finite existence.

While certain of Gide's works can be classified within the Tristan-Don Juan polarization, Gide's fiction is primarily a critical and ironic commentary on the dangers of authority and the pitfalls of freedom. Consequently, Gide places great emphasis on intellect and reason because reason alone, he insists, is capable of tempering both extremes.

2

The Symbolist Eagle

In 1891 Gide wrote a short piece only eight pages long entitled *Le Traité du Narcisse* and subtitled "theory of the symbol." The myth of a perfectly handsome Narcissus who fell in love with his own image as he contemplated its reflection on the clear surface of the spring waters may be taken as the symbol of a chaste and as yet virginal Gide whose books remain to be written. The Narcissus Gide is describing is someone who wants to know the form of his soul, someone who senses its beauty, someone who, like Rimbaud, has recognized himself a Poet. The work of art will be the image of his soul—an image purified and rarified so as to capture not only the dimensions of himself but the essence of a universal archetype. Gide's work will be the hieroglyph, each book a symbol of the Idea it contains. The archetype will become a dialogue of images—a dialogue of the soul—Narcissus' dialogue with his opposite reflection.

Flowers on the river bank, tree trunks, fragments of blue sky (Gide's Narcissus is looking at the flow of an ocean-bound river), a rapid series of images are colored by his eye and come into being only because he is there to register them. Narcissus marvels at the sequences, unable to determine whether it is his soul which guides the flow or whether it is the flow which guides his soul. All of these imperfect and constantly renewed forms, thinks Narcissus, are striving toward their first, paradisiac, crystalline, and now lost essence. And so, on the banks of his river, Narcissus dreams of a chaste Eden, a Garden of Ideas, a Paradise to be recreated.

Gide's Narcissus, like the Greek prototype, falls in love with his image, but the very gesture of desire that leans him toward the fragile reflection in the river brings him face to face with two lips and two staring eyes which immediately destroy the phantasmagoria of his dream. Gide the artist seems to be saying that he must not give in to narcissism, that he must not substitute desire for the task that lies ahead; that he must give expression to a vision or a dream and that, in order to do so, he must maintain objective distance and artistic detachment.

> Solemn and religious he resumes his calm attitude: he remains—a symbol growing bigger—and, as he leans over the appearance of the World, he feels vaguely within him, reabsorbed, the passing of the human generations (p. 11).[1]

A Gide-Narcissus in love with himself provides not only the basis for artistic tension but also the image of the Gidean dialogue. The "dialogues of Narcissus" are an aesthetic of love—more specifically self-love. Gide's reworking of the myth, typical of the manner in which he reworks Prometheus, or Oedipus, or Theseus, or the parable of the Prodigal Son stresses certain aspects of self-love as concern for the development of the self, in contrast to selfishness, egoism, and narcissism. Self-love is equated with self-realization.

The river in which Narcissus contemplates not only his image but the dream of Paradise is flowing toward the ocean, toward that expanse where the water, no longer contained by the two banks of the river, can mingle freely with the deep ocean currents. It is surely not by accident that Gide placed his Narcissus on the banks of a "fleuve," since an oceanbound river will enable the dialogue to "flow" toward its ultimate harmony in freedom and fulfillment.

Critics, generally, have interpreted *Le Voyage d'Urien* (1893) as Gide's renunciation of Symbolism. The "symbolism" Edmund Wilson describes in *Axel's Castle* does indeed seem to be the kind of chimera the irony of *voyage du rien* (of nothing) suggests. But is not this *nothing,* this deception which is the fruition of the journey, an elusive metaphor? Is it actually, as the critics of "symbolism" affirm, an attack on the dream-evasion from life, so typical of Axel, or, is it instead a tour de force of Symbolist technique which affirms no more than the fact that beauty lies in the pursuit and not in the finding? "We gave thanks to God for having hidden the goal from us, and for having deferred it so long that the only sure joy we had was in the efforts we made to reach it" (p. 64). Or that the exhilaration, as Pascal phrased it, is in the chase and not in the capture.

If this be true, and if man's happiness is not in the final discovery, but in the process of discovery, then perhaps *Le Voyage d'Urien* is not only the renunciation of Symbolism, but something far more interesting. This journey, reminiscent of a medieval romance, with its "envoi" dedicated to a protectress, in which the hero undertakes marvelous adventure for the sake of his "dame," does not lead him to the rose behind the garden wall but to the sterile wastes and black waters of a Polar Sea. It is not love Urien finds on the other side of the icecap, but once again, as in *Le Traité du Narcisse*, the image of his own reflection: "And kneeling down once more, we looked on the black water for the reflection of the sky which I am dreaming of" (p. 65). Or if it is love, it is Narcissus' brand of self-love, in this case, the artist's rapture for the beautiful image of his artistic achievement. Urien, like Narcissus leaning over the water, cannot possess his image because it was frozen in the ice outside the wall, and this frozen cadaver holding the white blank piece of paper (Mallarmé's white page?), is buried by the shores of the Polar Sea.

Just as Narcissus' attempt to kiss his own image destroys the illusion, so also Urien's voyage destroys the illusion. But of what? On the symbolic level, the cadaver in the ice, safely buried, does seem to represent Symbolism itself or at least the superficial kind of Symbolism which is often referred to as dream-evasion. The final "envoi," dedicated to the ephemeral feminine partner of this imaginary voyage, says that the story is no more than a lie, a dream, and that the journey was never made. Axel and his bride commit suicide after imagining together an exotic honeymoon rather than face the deception of reality, just as Des Esseintes tears up his ticket to London and returns to his apartment outside of Paris after eating a typical British meal. Since fantasy is capable of structuring all the pleasures of an imaginary reality why run the risk of an actual deception by confronting the imaginary with the real?

Such a substitution becomes the actual subject matter of much Symbolist literature and, like Narcissus kissing his image, destroys itself. The interesting aspect of Gide's piece, in addition to the fact that he abolishes the story at the end—a gesture typical of certain "new novels" by Beckett, Robbe-Grillet, Claude Ollier, and Didier Coste —is that it initiates the allegory of Gide's own artistic voyage. The dialogues of Narcissus are the artistic limits which frame the meaning of Gide's journey. His books put together—some more realistic, others less so—reveal the play of the imagination as it designs the vehicle with which to show the Idea behind the image, the universal concept behind the specific impression. It is the artist's role to force the reader to generalize from the specific and in so doing to unmask the meaning of the work of art. Gide was particularly adept at hiding meaning, in part because it depends upon the elucidation of the whole, but also because Gide recognized that his own private drama would only be palatable, artistically, if universalized in such a way as to encompass broader religious, philosophical, and psychological issues. The private drama, though latent in his works, did not burst forth until the publication of *Corydon* (1920 and 1924) which followed the burning of his letters by Madeleine in 1918. Perhaps, in the light of his drama, the final lines of the "envoi" assume particular meaning:

> *One day, as you know,*
> *I wished to look at life;*
> *we leaned towards things.*
> *But they seemed to me*
> *so serious, so terrible,*

> *so overwhelmingly responsible,*
> *that I dared not name them;*
> *I turned away—ah! My Lady—please forgive;*
> *I preferred to tell a lie.*
> *I was afraid to cry out*
> *lest I mar the poetry*
> *if I had told the Truth,*
> *the Truth which must be heard;*
> *preferring instead to lie still further*
> *and to wait—and wait, and wait . . .*
> *(pp. 66–67).*

The first edition of *Corydon* was not published until twenty-seven years later. This "delay" does indeed indicate a postponement of the "revelation," perhaps the "truth" Gide obliquely refers to in the "envoi." He appears to be subordinating the homosexual theme for the sake of his art, for fear of "spoiling the poetry." But such mysterious and veiled allusions can only refer to the problem which preoccupied him the most, a problem which is also at the heart of Narcissus' dialogue with himself and from which the more universal concepts emerge. Gide's art therefore will serve a dual purpose. It will polarize the conflict and the extremes he was so careful to cultivate, while at the same time it will deliberately mask the homosexual theme which seldom intrudes as openly as it does for example, in *Saül* (1903).

Narcissus' significant insight is to have known that the kiss (Gide's sexuality) would destroy his art. Narcissus' "kiss," as Gide anticipates its future manifestations, loses its narcissism. It is in the name of self-fulfillment (or self-love) that Gide launches his moral and artistic battle against the family, society, and religion. With this in mind *Le Voyage d'Urien* is not only the voyage of "nothing" but Gide's artistic exploration of the language of Symbolism in terms of his personal metaphor. That his muse Ellis, the Madame in the "envoi," should lead him to a frozen cadaver and the black waters of a Polar Sea, regardless of the beauties of the voyage, indicates that Gide will need a different language with which to affirm his artistic talent and personality. That he should unmask the Symbolists at their own game while masking his own homosexuality—which, at this period (1892), is by no means resolved—is no small achievement. Although *Le Voyage d'Urien* is not as good as his best work, it foreshadows an impressive talent, apparently sure of where it is going and what it expects to accomplish.

The story leaves no doubt as to its allegorical nature and intent. But what is this intent if it is more than a renunciation of Symbolism? More specifically, does it say anything about the Gidean "dialogue" and does it incorporate the artistic pattern of "extremes" so typical of the balance between *La Porte étroite* and *L'Immoraliste*?

Actually *Le Voyage d'Urien*, like Alissa's journey into asceticism, is a journey toward the divine city. But in order to reach the kingdom of God, Urien and his companion travelers must pass through lands of forbidden pleasure and regions of ennui. Only after having proved themselves worthy by resisting temptation on the islands of desire will they be ready for the ordeals of the austere Polar regions. The most difficult roads lead to the most exalted cities, says Urien, and if he and a few others resist the advances of Queen Haïatalnefus it is because of their "overwhelming desire for glorious actions" (p. 34). The Queen is not allowed to interfere with their lives and destiny—their presumed destiny being to reach the Pole. But in the light of what they find there and the disenchantment of having worked so hard for "nothing"—the divine city being nothing more than the black waters of the Polar Sea—the renunciation itself becomes meaningless. Ellis, who is sometimes a blonde woman and at other times a raven-haired vision dressed in white, is Urien's inspiration and the one who tells him that all roads lead to God. She becomes a seraphic being and ultimately ascends into heaven to join the other angels. This *white goddess* who incarnates the very attributes Robert Graves speaks of [2] shows Urien the beautiful silence of God in the Aurora Borealis. But beyond the flashy display of lights is a colorless dawn.

If the cadaver in the ice is a symbol for death and if the words HIC DESPERATUS, which the dead man inscribed over his icy tomb, are the same ones he might have inscribed (so Urien informs us) had he actually reached the "divine city," then the trip seems pointless. The narrative suggests that Urien should have perhaps succumbed to the women. The travelers might even have done so had it not been for the warning that "every climate has its dangers: every land its diseases. We had seen the plague on the mild islands; the languorous diseases near the marshes. A disease was now being born from the very absence of pleasurable sensations" (p. 56). Scurvy is the sickness of the Polar regions. Urien speaks of dangers lurking everywhere but perhaps none so misleading as those which emerge from the stagnant waters of the Sargasso Sea. These waters lead the passengers up the river of ennui. It is on the banks of this river that Urien finds Ellis who later appears to him in the form of a white diaphanous woman. It is at this stage in the journey that the men see the twelve sheep in an apocalyptic vision worthy of Blake. It is significant that these dreamlike encounters should emerge from the regions of ennui where the river inexplicably begins to flow in its opposite direction like a story being read backwards.

This mysterious river which flows simultaneously in both directions seems to be the meeting point of the extremes—the middle ground where they join and from which equally accessible but contradictory courses of action are possible. In other words the river of ennui can lead either to the tropical islands of desire or to the polar regions of religious asceticism: the two poles of Gide's artistic dialogue and the regions in which eagles are bred.

Urien will explain the purpose of his voyage as the search for revealing acts: "You set out one morning, because you have learned in your studies that you must manifest what you are; you go out into the world in search of revealing actions—and who can tell what dark valley joins the world in which you live to our [sic] upper room in which you dream" (p. 45). The illogical appearance and disappearance of landscapes and people is the dream to be deciphered; it is the clue to the meaning of Urien's acts bound together, as they are, by the varying lights of many dawns: a voyage which begins at dawn, moves through the "shivering and suffering dawn" of ennui, and is finally climaxed by the false dawn of the Aurora Borealis only to be resolved at last by a "colorless dawn." How different from the beginning when dawns are anticipated as the "surprises of seas, oriental lights, whose dream or remembrance, at night, haunted our fastidious studying with a desire for travel!" (p. 15).

It is appropriate that the name Urien should resemble the name of the ship Orion on which he and six other travelers embark; that the constellation of Orion has seven stars and that Urien is one of seven companions to reach the Pole; that Orion in Greek is also a play on words meaning urine and that Orion, the giant, emerged from the ground nine months after three gods took the hide of a heifer, urinated on it and buried it. Urien and Urine are surely close enough to justify some scatological inference in view of the play on "Urien." Orion was a hunter and Urien is hunting for the meaning of his acts. The ship Orion will carry Urien to the divine city in the heart of the Polar wastes where he finds nothing.

Le Voyade d'Urien does not seem to be a renunciation of symbols, since the whole work is symbolic, but a critique of that "divine city" lodged in the Polar wastes. Urien's voyage, like Alissa's, is indeed an austere journey toward a dubious kingdom.

Another work, *La Tentative amoureuse* (1893), subtitled in 1899 as *The Treatise of Vain Desire*, suggests that while desire may not exactly be vain, it is certainly ephemeral and capricious. Luc's and Rachel's love consumes itself—a consummation which breeds familiarity, ennui, and the boredom of surprises that are no longer tantalizing. It is a boredom of happiness devoid of expectation. Objects of desire are like perishable concretions which disintegrate the moment they are touched. They need to be dispersed and replaced by new desires and new goals so that the self may go beyond the stagnation of ennui, develop new horizons, and evolve new insights in the process of self-fulfillment.

The need of the self to go beyond the stagnation of ennui and to develop new horizons, while expounded briefly in *La Tentative amoureuse* (1893), is explored in detail in *Paludes* (1895). In a sense *Narcisse, Le Voyage d'Urien, La Tentative amoureuse,* and *Paludes* form a quartet, each work supplementing, complementing, and explaining the other. We identify the narrator of *Paludes* with Tityrus who, like Narcissus, is looking at his reflection in the river. *Paludes*' narrator creates a duplicate image of himself but with a heightened artistic realism. The ennui of the Sargasso Sea which Urien traverses is the same ennui and stagnation of Tityrus' swamps. The potentially closed world of *La Tentative amoureuse* is the closed world of *Paludes* which reappears again briefly in *Le Prométhée mal enchaîné* (1899).

Though symbolic in structure and professed intent these works are highly critical of the Symbolism of Mallarmé's salon on which Gide was nurtured. As critical works they are also ironic ones and it is inherent within the Gidean dialectic that he must pursue an idea to its logical conclusion and, therefore, exaggerate it. Within the authoritarian-humanistic opposition, Symbolism and master Symbolists of the late nineteenth century seem to have exerted an artistic authoritarianism comparable to Madame Gide's austerity and religious dogma against which Gide was rebelling. Nevertheless the same fascination which prompts him to explore Alissa's asceticism, manifests itself initially in an exploration of the inherent possibilities of Symbolism. Gide's hostility to Symbolism, though latent in the works discussed in this chapter, manifests itself quite openly in *Paludes* and finally explodes into an affirmation of things and reality in *Les Nourritures terrestres* (1897).

But before launching into his exuberant description of the North African landscape Gide first explored the possibility and renunciation of such a visit. The narrator of *Paludes,* like Des Esseintes and Axel, talks persuasively of leaving the city for the freedom of the open road, for the wide open spaces of the country, even for North Africa itself. Like Des Esseintes returning to his apartment, and like Axel, the narrator-Tityrus commits moral suicide by remaining in Paris in order to write *Polders*, a new work which, we presume, will be just like *Paludes*.

Paludes represents the stagnation, the impasse, and the absurdity of the Symbolism Gide was reacting to. The hero of *Paludes* succumbs to a death of the soul in contrast to the plenitude of *Les Nourritures* which exalts the present, freedom from the past, and the need to escape the stifling oppression of inner rooms. Gide, ever conscious of the influence a work of art exerts on its creator, wrote in his *Journal* in August of 1893 apropos of *La Tentative amoureuse*:

> I wanted to suggest . . . the influence of the book on the person writing it, and during that very writing. As the book issues from us, it changes us, it modifies the course of our life; . . . I was particularly sad because a dream of unfulfillable joy was tormenting me. I tell this dream and, isolating the joy from the dream, I make it mine; my dream has broken the spell; I am full of joy.[3]

Anachronistically, in *Paludes*, Gide denies his narrator the privilege of liberation because he, Gide, needs it for himself. What happens, therefore, is that the narrator who is writing a book about a satisfied Tityrus contemplating the swamps from his tower, becomes that very Tityrus "who smiles" benignly and without dissatisfaction on his human situation. The narrator, unable or unwilling to purge himself of the Symbolist ennui succumbs to it while Gide performs the necessary catharsis in order to escape its deadly poison.

It is the simultaneity of the two stories, the narrator's and Tityrus', one presumably real, the other fictitious, that establishes their curious identity. The fiction of *Paludes* serves to stress, by contrast and, as the narrator says, by artistic concentration and heightened intensity of emotion, the reality and realism of the other. Yet the two overlap, and the ennui of daily minutiae and the trivia of existence, all of those factors which inhibit the development of the self—Richard's marriage to a woman he does not love, his fostering of six children, the unimaginative and perhaps necessary routine of doing things every day in exactly the same way, even sinking into mediocrity—these are some of the inhibiting elements of *Paludes*. There are more. Gide suggests there are as many variations as there are people and that each man is capable of surrounding himself or being enveloped by an environment which is equally destructive to the self. The literary salon he parodies is in itself a parody of the Symbolist salon Gide knew. The *Paludes* he defines, as "the story of a bachelor in a tower surrounded by marshes," is the archetype not only of a Symbolism that had reached an impasse but of a universal and prostrate man, man "recubans." At the end of *Paludes*, the narrator, like Richard, assumes the self-effacing task of those who are "humble" and care for the needy and less fortunate.

But this Nietzschean theme, present already in Gide and which he develops in *L'Immoraliste*, forms part of the Gidean spectrum of values. There is reference to freedom, the gratuitous act, the need to disquiet or trouble ("inquiéter"), and the urgent call to life itself. The narrator's refusal to recognize these Gidean values, comparable to Edouard's refusal to incorporate Boris' "suicide" into his *Faux-Monnayeurs*, is in itself a condemnation by the author. The narrator's decision to write another *Paludes* in *Polders* contrasts with the quality of Gide's next work, *Les Nourritures terrestres*, thereby stressing an important difference between Gide and the narrator.

The theme of the oppressed inner self is more fully developed now. *La Tentative amoureuse* stressed the need for escape from routine toward the unexpected. *Le Voyage d'Urien* attacked not only Symbolism but the meaninglessness of religious asceticism. *Paludes'* attack is even sharper for it is rooted in a realism absent from the previous narratives. The dreamlike timelessness of a mythological setting has been replaced by an identifiable reality. The narrator who moves in a city we can recognize and who speaks with living men and women rather than with archetypes of a dream, not only frames his attack in more realistic terms, like Flaubert moving from the vision-ary sequences of *La Tentation de Saint Antoine* to *Madame Bovary*, but identifies certain social forces destructive to the self, not yet as fully identified as they will be in *Les Faux-Monnayeurs*, but nevertheless exposed.

3

The Immoral Gate

Two of the fattest eagles in Gide's sky soar appreciatively over the heads of Michel in *L'Immoraliste* (1902) and Alissa in *La Porte étroite* (1909). They feed frequently on the exposed livers of these two protagonists and sate themselves on Michel's "diseased" passion for freedom as well as on Alissa's "heroic" but futile asceticism.

The "gate" through which Alissa forces herself is immoral because it negates life (hers). Michel's freedom, which would intensify the living process, becomes immoral because, it too, ultimately, negates life (Marceline's). It is the excesses of both which are immoral, a point of contact where the *extremes touch*.

While Gide criticism has recognized the antipodal nature of these two works, elucidation often focuses on one of several levels of meaning. Alissa's asceticism is opposed to Michel's immoralism. Her sacrifice of self contradicts his sacrifice of Marceline, his wife. Alissa's narrowing freedom of choice corresponds to his expanding possibilities for choice. Her religious austerity vies with his Nietzschean "disponibilité." But none of these levels necessarily excludes the others, any more than Michel's incipient homosexuality negates the rational basis of his "immoralism." Alissa's fear of becoming like her mother, a woman of the flesh, does not exclude, but rather supports the voice of an authoritarian conscience which would narrow life's road, eliminate temptation, and discard beauty.

We can and, for the sake of analysis, we must isolate each level, but once the pans of water from the living stream have been scrutinized, to use Bergson's image, we must pour the contents back into the river lest the arbitrary separation distort or exaggerate the meaning of each. It is the flow, the process of becoming which Gide stressed so often, that gives his work its beauty, its complexity, and its contradictions.

Michel, in the name of spontaneity, sincerity, and self-fulfillment will sever all ties and all bonds with material possessions: his land, his money, and his wife, in a passionate effort at some kind of ultimate liberation, only to conclude that it is not freeing oneself, but knowing what to do with one's freedom that counts. The incipient homosexual theme (which Guérard has analyzed so well), skillfully and cleverly handled, and which time and again lends verisimilitude to Michel's behavior, remains subordinate (as Brée points out) to the more important and more generalized theme of spiritual and philosophical emancipation. Michel's ennui stems from the fact that, after liberating himself, he does not know how to use his freedom. He is "blind" to the consequences of his behavior. This blindness, this passion for freedom, regardless of the consequences to others, is his eagle. But the book, by exposing Michel's daring, as well as his limitations, serves, as Northrop Frye has indicated, in lieu of experience and, hopefully, will prevent a similar blindness in us.

Blindness (moral as well as physical) is one of the metaphors which links not only *L'Immoraliste* and *La Porte étroite* but also *La Symphonie pastorale, Oedipe, Robert,* and *Les Faux-Monnayeurs.* Gertrude's blindness in *La Symphonie pastorale,* like Oedipus', is the analogue for other states of spiritual, psychic, or emotional myopia from which so many of Gide's characters are suffering. Gide taps the elusive and subtle currents of the self, exposes the flaws, and reveals the ratiocinations that hide the flaws.

The flaw is woven, as Gide intended, into a *critical* and *ironic* theorem whose purpose, in Alissa's case, is to demonstrate the consequences of her error of judgment and the magnitude of the deception imposed upon the self.

Her death reveals the incredible resourcefulness of the psyche which would rationalize behavior, spiritualize desire, and kill the body in order to protect an ideal which Gide, in the final analysis, exposes as false.

Gide takes Alissa's basic flaw, adds an austere puritanism as a catalyst, supplies the necessary characters for dramatic interest, and then weaves the fabric of his fiction from the psychic contradictions with which he himself is so familiar. As Gide describes the process, he starts with an abstract idea and then animates the characters within a pre-established framework. What is not always evident in this creative process, is Gide's ability, like God creating Eve, to draw ribs from his own body which he then animates with breath. These are characters who subsequently embody most if not all of his subtle, nuanced, contradictory, and elusive personality. One psychological dimension slides into another and unless the reader retains the premises of the theorem, which are clearly indicated at the outset, it is easy to be "misled" by the rationalizations behind which the characters hide their true motives.

But what, in the case of *L'Immoraliste*, are the premises? First, during Michel's youth and after the death of his devoutly Protestant mother, an atheist father devotedly cares for and faithfully instructs the son. Second, Michel, out of pity and without loving her, marries Marceline to please his dying father. Five years after his mother's death, at the age of twenty, Michel is so learned and so erudite that he is ready to collaborate with his father who publishes *L'Essai sur les cultes phrygiens*, for which Michel has done most of the work. The reviews are favorable and the father, deliberately, takes credit for the article. At the time Michel says only that he was confused by such fraudulent behavior. The "immoral" seed seems to have been sown, however, and the father's success will provide an ironic lesson for a son who, later, will blithely poach against himself while deceiving everyone else on his estate.

At twenty-five Michel is still a precocious adolescent who knows nothing about life and who has rarely looked at anything but ruins and books. Michel also informs us (the clue is critical) that his Puritan childhood has taught him to hate weakness and abandon. Therefore, when he coughs and Marceline faints at the sight of his blood, he rushes angrily to pick her up: "Wasn't it enough for *me* to be ill?" (p. 379).[1] Nevertheless, Michel is grateful to his wife for the love and care she lavishes upon him. But he is less impressed by her devotion than by the implications of his own experience.

> The important thing was that death had brushed me, as they say, with its wing. The important thing was that it seemed to me astonishing that I was alive, that days took on for me an unhoped—for light. Before, I thought, I did not understand that I was living (p. 381).

Michel marvels at the "beautiful health" radiating from the bodies of the North African Arab boys and, in comparing his own ugly black blood to the redness of Bachir's, he discovers in himself a sudden rage to live

> live! I want to live. I want to live. I clenched my teeth, my fists, concentrated my whole being wildly, desolately, in this effort toward existence (p. 383).

There are obvious and striking parallels between Michel and Roquentin in Sartre's *La Nausée*. Even without analyzing the similarities in detail it is fair to say that *L'Immoraliste* sets the stage for the "existential" themes, not only of Sartre, but of Malraux and Camus as well. Roquentin's consciousness of *existence* and the thematic repetition of the noun, as well as the verb *to exist*, corresponds to Michel's discovery that he too has a special identity. Roquentin abandons the obscure biography he had been writing, just as Michel reorients his entire attitude toward books and the past. While Michel's evolving freedom surpasses in audacity anything Roquentin can envision, the philosophical question posed by Michel's "dreadful freedom" will be the preoccupation of Sartre's philosophical writings as well as of his fictional heroes.

Michel cultivates his will power and, in his struggle for life against death, directs his hostility toward everything that inhibits recovery. He rejects prayer, Marceline's pious invocations, and God's help because, he says, he does not want to be indebted to anyone (Damocles' eagle was his feeling of indebtedness), even to God, particularly to God. Do not such behavior and such attitudes postulate a desire for total self-reliance? This exclusive responsibility to the self is expressed in terms of an animal vitality, in terms of a biological need for survival which leaves no room or time for moral growth. Michel speaks at length of his body and refers to his neglect of the "mind" because he does not yet have the strength for what he calls a "double life" and a dual rehabilitation. It is this primary negligence which explains the nature and direction of his subsequent moral development.

Yet paralleling his purely physical recovery we witness not only a discovery of beauty and life but a new and acute consciousness of death:

> I was horrified by this calm; and suddenly I was over-whelmed once again, as if to protest, to assert itself, to grieve in silence, the sense of the tragedy of my life, so violent, sorrowful almost, and so impetuous that I would have cried out, if I could have cried out like an animal (p. 396).

It is this existential awareness of death which, as it does for the heroes of Sartre and Camus, now activates Michel's appreciation of life. His poaching against himself negates certain traditional values and plunges us into an experience of the absurd which he himself calls by that name (p. 453).

But Gide is never abstract. Psychological verisimilitude, even to the detail of father plagiarizing the work of his son, contributes to and explains the origins as well as the step-by-step progression of Michel's moral philosophy. The past is identified with the "immobility of death." What matters is the present. His erudition interferes now with his joy. In a typical succession of antiromantic statements he says that he hates death, ruins, and melancholy. He has the feeling at last that he has discovered an authentic being—an inner core which books, teachers, parents, and even he himself had, at first, tried to suppress (pp. 398–99). From this moment on he despises that former "secondary being." He now systematically begins the destruction of everything that had been superimposed on that interior being which he calls the "authentic self."

> And I compared myself to the palimpsests; I tasted the joy of the scholar, who, under more recent writings, uncovers, on the same paper, a very ancient text infinitely more precious. What was this occult text? In order to read it, was it not necessary first of all to eradicate the more recent ones? (p. 399).

Reminiscent of *Les Nourritures terrestres* is Michel's renaissance in the North African landscape, this plunge into the pool by the waterfall, and the drying and the rubbing of his limbs with sprigs of mint. Every day, he feels, he is advancing toward a richer, fuller, and more savory existence. The concluding sentence of Part I describes Michel's preparations for happiness. Parts II and III will tell of its destruction.

In the meantime all augurs well. Michel, after his return to France, takes great interest in the management of his farms. But his "return from the dead" makes him feel like a "stranger" even among his friends. This ennui and restlessness are not redirected until his encounter with Ménalque who seeks an exaltation rather than a diminution of life. He cultivates Michel's new moral self and imbues him with the notion of a Nietzschean "disponibilité." So the doctrine of moral and intellectual freedom and self-fulfillment grafts itself onto the stem of physical rehabilitation on which Michel has fastened all his energy and enthusiasm. Meanwhile the incrustations of a Puritan morality have been erased, and, along with the biological élan toward health, we now have a self-centered, single-minded philosophical emphasis on total and irrevocable self-fulfillment.

But Michel's consumption, like Alissa's fear of sensuality, has left an emotional scar which colors his view of reality. We could understand and perhaps forgive a Puritan morality which equates cleanliness with Godliness, but Michel's overreaction to spots and dirt will contaminate his relationship with Marceline after she, in turn, gets tuberculosis, since he will react to her as a "chose abîmée," a worn out and spoiled object.

> A glass of curaçao had been spilled on the carpet. Albert's muddy shoes, as he lay impudently on a couch, were soiling the cover. And the dust that we were breathing in came from the horrible wear-and-tear of things . . . I had a sudden frantic urge to shove all my guests out the door. Furniture, fabrics, prints, upon the first *stain* [my italics] lost all value for me; stained things, things *marked by illness and designated for death* [my italics] (p. 430).

Will not Michel's pathological reaction to stains and, by association, to death, including the spot on Marceline's lungs, condemn her? Will not his diabolical trek south through Italy to North Africa, weaken, gradually exhaust, and kill her? Michel's final act of liberation and self-fulfillment is performed and consummated at her expense. "The sickness had entered Marceline, from then on lived in her, marked her, stained her. She was a thing now gutted" (p. 439).

But Michel's behavior is too flagrant in its contradiction. On the one hand he claims to be acting in the name of a new-found freedom while, on the other, he is acting compulsively and in such a way as to negate the very premises he has espoused: "I was like someone possessed" (p. 459). He mistakes the debauchery of bums for spontaneity and goes "slumming" in the name of sincerity. It is the *emotional scar* of his brush with death, an *atrophied sense of morality*, and a *pathological reaction to stains* which now negate his newly found freedom. Nor can Michel stand being indebted to Marceline for helping to cure him. He will, perhaps subconsciously, eliminate her rather than live with the obligation, since an indebtedness of this kind (as Damocles found out) is a great inhibitor of freedom. And so, the closer the ties, the greater the resentment and the more flagrant his plunge into debauchery: "The society of the lowest order of men was delectable company to me" (p. 463).

Although the dominant theme of *L'Immoraliste* is Michel's pursuit of absolute freedom, his inability to cope with his freedom, once it has been realized, does not negate the theme itself. What Gide seems to be saying, instead, is that the flaws in Michel's personality will distort and warp his use of freedom in such a way as to denature it. His excesses, even his "crime," are not necessarily the product of freedom as much as they are a reflection of its misuses. Also, the manner in which Gide traces the origins, progression, and climax of the story reveals the subordinate themes which blend effortlessly into the whole. The homosexual theme, intimated in the beginning, becomes overt and, by the time Michel embraces the driver of the phaeton, there is little doubt about his leanings.

A preference for men or boys does not, in itself, explain Michel's sacrifice of Marceline. Nevertheless, it will be one of the rings in the chain, linked to that "aberration," "obstinate blindness," and "voluntary madness" (p. 462) which goad him toward a renewed pursuit of the light and heat of Biskra. "But," asks Michel, "was I master of my will? and captain of my desires?" (p. 462). In his journey south through Italy toward North Africa in search of who knows what answers, Michel leaves Switzerland because he is too bored by that "honest country" (p. 458).[2] The question of honesty now relates to the problem of sincerity and spontaneity and with the same kind of "rage" (a key word in the narrative) with which he leaves Switzerland (a vertiginous descent into Italy with overtones of the Biblical "fall"), he follows through with his mad and not entirely unconscious annihilation of Marceline.

This impulsive traveling was tiring Marceline; but what tired her still more, I am not afraid now to admit it, was the fear of what was in my mind. "I understand," she told me one day, "I quite understand your doctrine—for it has

now become a doctrine. It is a beautiful one, perhaps, . . .
but it excludes the weak" (pp. 459–60).

Michel has become the exponent of Nietzsche's polemi-
cal doctrine stressing the inherent and aristocratic superiority of the strong who must not allow themselves to be
downgraded by the weak. But even if he does exorcise his
inner demon Michel is not entirely convinced of the
moral validity of his act:

> I have freed myself, perhaps; but so what? I am suffering
> from this purposeless freedom. It is not, believe me, that I
> am tired of my crime, if you choose to call it that—but I
> must prove to myself that I have not overstepped my rights
> (p. 471).

This philosophical theme, with its Nietzschean and existential overtones, finally dominates the homosexual one.
Michel's severing of all ties with the past, monetary, social, intellectual, and emotional corresponds to the quick-
ening tempo of his madness and his blind rush toward a
nebulous future which he fully longs for but which, when
it comes, he will not fully comprehend. He has discarded
every tie that might possibly inhibit his freedom. He is a
free agent and he alone is responsible for his actions. No
code of ethics, be it the Church, or society, or the family,
or the internalized voice of God or parents acts upon him.
Michel is free in the sense that he is neither influenced by
nor submits to any a priori morality which might modify
his behavior. He and he alone decides, acts upon, and
abides by the consequences of his choices. In Sartrian
vocabulary he defines himself through choice and we now
know him as the *Immoralist*, rather than as the *Amoralist*.

Since authors select their titles carefully, the nuance is
perhaps significant. Gide, if he really approved or identified with Michel should have used the nonloaded title,
amoral. But Michel, even from Gide's point of view, is
immoral.

In discarding the layers of social values and in peeling
off the incrustations of external morality, he has exposed
his "moi profond," presumably untouched and no longer

to be influenced by anything outside himself. If this inner core were inherently good, as Rousseau affirmed, then the ultimate freedom he achieved should have been a source of great joy, comparable to the enthusiasm of the narrator in *Les Nourritures*. Michel is *not* happy. He is depressed and overwhelmed by a feeling of emptiness.

The different themes, so skillfully interwoven, all move toward and explain Michel's "failure." But the moral, philosophical, and religious overtones (content) blend into form and are part of an inevitable artistic dimension which makes *L'Immoraliste* work for the reader. The very title suggests a flouting of accepted values. Michel's behavior, moreover, confirms the worst expectations of a bourgeois reader, insomuch as he attacks God, money, marriage, landed gentry, erudition, stability, veneration of the past and its traditions, in short, every major societal cornerstone. One is tempted to conclude that the fight against the vast forces of the social structure is futile. But this is probably not true. The obstacles to Michel's success are not society's insomuch as he succeeds in abolishing everything he set out to destroy. It is his own inner obstacle he cannot overcome. It is the stain inside which contaminates and then undermines the freedom he has so desperately conquered. His passion feeds his eagle and keeps it airborne.

If *L'Immoraliste* is the exploration of an excess in one direction, *La Porte étroite* is an exploration of an excess in the opposite. As in *L'Immoraliste* the levels of meaning are constantly shifting. Like Michel, Alissa has an inner scar and an emotional trauma. Michel's lust for life fears weakness and disease, while Alissa's wish for the absolute is, in reality, fear of life. Sainthood via the "strait gate" is more important in the long run than marriage to Jérome. In his presence, lest she succumb to his advances, she is hostile, rigid, cold, and forbidding. Her beauty must be mutilated by a severe hairdo, plain clothes, and menial sock mending. She removes the books of poetry from her shelves, all reminders of Jérome, and replaces them with trashy religious treatises. Even when Jérome kisses her she manages a "have pity on us"—words which drop Jérome to his knees, a position from which he can, once again, worship the Madonna of his love. The spirit triumphs.

Such behavior is consistent with Denis de Rougement's interpretation which places this novel within the framework of the Tristan Myth. In fact the "obstacle" which keeps Tristan's and Iseult's love alive governs Alissa's and Jérome's relationship. She uses her sister Juliette as an obstacle to marriage. She then arbitrarily imposes a waiting period on future marriage plans, arbitrarily forbids Jérome from visiting her and then, while he is in the army, writes love letters to him in which she confesses her eternal devotion. She also believes in their union after death which will not be consummated, she thinks, if it is realized on earth. Since the union after death is so much more important and is "forever," the words "have pity on us" (my italics) explain why succumbing to the immediate desires of the flesh would destroy their marriage in heaven. The obstacles, therefore, logically correspond to her moments of greater longing. Jérome's agreement to leave the moment Alissa removes the little amethyst cross is symbolic not only of a profound understanding between the two, but also of the cause for which she is asking him to leave.

It is not marriage with Jérome she dreads but the possibility that, once her senses are aroused, she will not be able to resist the imperious lure of other men. She would rather die, since it is this fear of a weak "fiber" within which leads her to reject earthly happiness. The tragedy of her flaw or her blindness is that she dies alone, on the verge of blasphemy, deserted, she feels, by the very God for whom she has sacrificed her life.

The small gate in the garden wall is the visual correlative of her dilemma. Its very narrowness symbolizes her withdrawal from the world as well as her aspirations toward an afterlife. Yet the flimsy latch on the inside reveals how easily Jérome might have pushed through her resistance had he chosen to venture beyond her contrived barriers. The presence of this "gate" through which she thinks she must pass in order to be worthy of the beyond is a constant reminder not only of the sermon of the "strait gate," but of the torments she must suffer in order to force herself through its narrow aperture. Like Damocles, she dies doing it. The "strait gate" is her eagle.

Gide's narrative exposes the ambivalence of Alissa's feelings. It is hard to emphasize Alissa's emotional scar over concern for her sister's welfare unless, of course, we begin to suspect the motives of altruism. Gide demonstrates again, as he did in *L'Immoraliste*, the elusive nature of human motivation and the shifting sands of the human psyche. In the light of Alissa's subsequent behavior, namely her sacrifice of earthly happiness for the sake of heavenly joy, her willingness to give Juliette "first crack" at Jérome is not as selfless as it first appears. Alissa's death, a rare enough event, confirms not only the violence of the struggle between the spirit and the flesh, but also the extremity she has had to force upon herself in order to guarantee entry into heaven.

Claudel's interpretation of *La Porte étroite*, was quite appropriate, insofar as he saw in Alissa the embodiment of an extreme Protestantism. A Catholic woman with Alissa's religious propensities would have, no doubt, become a nun. It is Alissa's personal, rather than Church-oriented dialogue with God which, according to Claudel, leads to her distortion of values and eventual moral helplessness.[3]

If we believe that aberrations of the self, whether physical or spiritual, are wrong, then we must conclude that Alissa's self-destruction was, in the final analysis, accomplished by the voice of her authoritarian conscience.

Yet to liberate oneself from authoritarian systems is, in itself, no guarantee of a satisfactory solution, as Michel's dilemma clearly indicates. The voice of the humanistic conscience, though perhaps no longer contaminated by values external to the self may, as in Michel's case, be sick. An early trauma and the complexities of living impose inordinate demands on the personality which it may or may not be able to solve or assimilate. Thus Michel, in the process of recovering from his nearly fatal illness, and in his determination to heal the body, kills all vestiges of moral responsibility. He listens exclusively to what may be described as a humanistic conscience but his compulsive attitude toward stains, his latent homosexuality, and a newly discovered Nietzschean ethic interfere with the "true" expression of his inner self.

Michel succeeds physically but fails morally. While Gide obviously approves of his physical recovery, he is critical of his inability to resolve the problem of human freedom. Michel, like the characters in Sartre's *Huis Clos*, is at an impasse. He too is in hell and suffering because, in his unbridled pursuit of self-liberation, he has failed to resolve the problem of the confrontation of the self with other selves, a confrontation which inevitably postulates their freedom as well as his.

There are pitfalls in listening to the humanistic conscience (Michel) just as there are dangers in listening to the distorted voice of God (Alissa). While Gide prefers the humanistic to the authoritarian conscience he is not unaware of the falsifications and contaminations which may occur in both. Must not Michel, in his search for an absolute freedom, liberate himself completely from any vestige of authority, even God's? Must he not since Marceline is a believer and since she prays, demonstrate that his own *human* power for survival is stronger than God's care for her, or for the weak in general? Such a motive must surely explain why he repeatedly and almost violently thrusts the rosary into Marceline's hand during the last moments of her agony. The rosary, as the symbol of God's presence or absence, must remain with her to the bitter end. She has been Michel's guinea pig. His search for knowledge was stronger than any love or affection he might have had for her.

In the end he can only wonder if he has not overstepped the bounds of human freedom or, as he calls them, his rights. The concentration camp executioner in Hochhuth's *The Deputy* speaks eloquently, as Michel might have but does not, of God's silence and of His unwillingness or inability to help victims in distress. The death by plague of the small boy in Camus' *La Peste* is also designed to demonstrate God's "absence" and impotence.

Michel has proved that he can sever all ties and even kill, but his remorse, if indeed we can call it that, does not reflect shame, or fear, or sadness, any more than does the reaction of Hochhuth's executioner who comments on the discrepancy between his own horrible acts and the cosmic silence. Now that Michel has demonstrated what he wants to know he has called three friends to whom he is "confessing" his moral dilemma only because he suspects that he may have gone too far.

But the question of rights is, perhaps, not the real issue. *L'Immoraliste* is an important book because in it Michel wrestles with the same problems Kirilov does in *The Possessed*. Kirilov commits suicide in order to prove that he is free and that God does not exist. But by committing suicide he fails to live the consequences of his freedom. Michel, like Raskolnikov and Lafcadio must prove to himself that he can kill and live with the consequences because to flout tradition and convention and remain alive is the ultimate test of human freedom.

Freedom is an elusive goal, however. Perhaps we should not condemn Michel's search but only his excesses just as we admire Alissa's heroism but condemn its futility. Alissa's brand of Protestantism can only lead to a self-destructive impasse unless, of course, we believe in Tristan and his eagle.

4

The Pastoral Symphony

In the March 8 entry to his journal the Pastor writes that
he is recording "the story of Gertrude's moral and intellectual development." But his analysis of the blind girl's
progress parallels the exposé of his own emotional cecity.

It is Gertrude's adoption which leads to the polarization
of attitudes in the Pastor's family and to the resultant
conflict and tragedy. It is a conflict which begins as a
father's opposition to his son's marriage, which then
evolves into a dialogue between Christ and St. Paul, and
which finally metamorphoses into a Protestant-Catholic
discord. On a philosophic level it is, once again, the dialogue between freedom and submission to authority.

In keeping with one of his artistic devices Gide has
snuffed out the buds he does not want to flower and in
nourishing four character-buds—the Pastor, Gertrude,
Jacques (the Pastor's son), and Amélie (the Pastor's
wife)—Gide has grown his usual, and I use Justin
O'Brien's term, "monstrous" plant. But instead of his
customary method, which in both *La Porte étroite* and in
L'Immoraliste produced one enormous flower, he has
grown four smaller ones. Furthermore, the ethical framework of the Michel-Alissa "dialogue" now exists within
one work and the resultant artistic tension, as in *Saül*, is
self-contained.

Gide's classicism is here apparent. As in Racinian tragedy, this "récit" moves logically and inevitably toward
dissension, antagonism, and death. Thus, the adoption of
Gertrude will, in the course of two years and ten months,

lead to her suicide, Jacques' conversion, and the Pastor's moral crisis. Her blindness, her innocence, and her beauty will precipitate and expose actions and thoughts so disturbing to the Pastor that he will write a journal in order to clarify and understand them. Gertrude's beauty and intelligence will lead him and his son to fall in love with her, so that what began as charitable love for a poor, helpless orphan transforms itself into carnal desire, the implications of which neither she nor the pastor can escape. Gertrude will become the focal point for tension and hostility between the Pastor and his family.

The Pastor acts in the name of Gertrude's moral and intellectual development but in indulging her he offends his wife and alienates his son irrevocably. Jacques' resultant disillusion with his father, his frustrated love for Gertrude, and a newly discovered religious zeal lead him to destroy the framework which his father has built into Gertrude's view of reality. From Gertrude's physical blindness the Pastor concludes that she must remain blind to sin and evil because exposure to ugliness would mar the inner beauty of her soul. "I had not dared," says the Pastor, "speak to Gertrude of evil, sin, and death." He wishes to keep her in a primordial state of innocence and purity. In spite of his allusion to and rejection of the father's similar role in Dickens' *Cricket on the Hearth*, the Pastor, who no doubt thinks he can succeed where others have failed, structures an environment for Gertrude unsullied by the contradictions and impurities of reality.

It is difficult to say at exactly what stage of his thinking the Pastor's rationalization about moral blindness evolves into actual complicity, although it corresponds roughly to the division of the book into two parts—the "first notebook" and the "second notebook." The first two months of the journal describe the past, beginning the narrative two years and six months after Gertrude has joined the family. The last two months of the journal deal with the present and lead directly to Gertrude's conversion and death.

It is the operation on Gertrude's eyes which symbolically opens her moral vision and exposes the ugliness and the sin which the Pastor had so carefully been hiding from her. She sees pain and suffering on Amélie's face caused, she feels, by their "sin." She never imagined, she says, that men's brows could be so bony nor that there was so much suffering. In shielding her from evil the Pastor has made her doubly vulnerable. She is unprepared morally and intellectually to cope with the complex reality the operation on her eyes will reveal. Nor does Jacques help matters by reading her the passages from the Bible which his father had deliberately kept from her. One passage in St. Paul, in particular, will assume an extraordinary meaning for her and will precipitate her suicide: "For I was alive without the law once; but when the commandment came, sin revived, and I died."

And so, overwhelmed by guilt and caught in a web of contradictions she cannot resolve, she loses the will to live and dies with her moral and intellectual fibers literally torn asunder. She feels responsible for the pain she has caused Amélie. She is grateful to the Pastor for his care and the love which has made her development possible. Spiritually she loves the Pastor, but physically, it is Jacques' face she loves: "When I saw Jacques, I suddenly realized that it was not you I loved, but him. He had your face, exactly: I mean the one I imagined you as having" (May 29). Gertrude's conflict has thus been intensified, since on May 18 she tells the Pastor that she cannot stop loving him. During the night of May 19 their lips actually meet. Blind, Gertrude loves the Pastor, but with her eyes open she loves a face which, were it not for the Pastor's age, might still have attracted her. Her love for the father and for the son is now a two-headed Janus—one side contradicting the other; one representing "good," the other "evil." She loves both men and must, inevitably, hate them both since the Pastor's values negate Jacques' values.

Gide cleverly plays a scale of antitheses which, contrapuntally, emphasize, or perhaps contribute to the musical "structure" of the book. It is not my purpose to describe the thematic resemblances between Gide's and Beethoven's pastoral symphonies. There are similarities even though, as Thibaudet observes, Gide's pastoral, in its "austerity," when contrasted with *Les Faux-Monnayeurs,* is more like a sonata than a symphony. What interests us here is not the fact that four months of the Pastor's journal correspond roughly to the four movements of a symphony (even though Beethoven's pastoral symphony has five), or that Gide, like a composer, built his work on a theme consisting of four notes supplied by two tones — that is the Pastor, Gertrude, Jacques, and Amélie (the four notes), all functioning within a world in which good and evil (the two tones) coexist — or that he begins with a statement of a theme in concentrated form and then reveals the nature of the theme by elaborating the "symphonic" thought.

What interests us is the nature of the elaboration, the interplay of white and black and the resultant absence or presence of color which captures the moral opposition between Jacques and the Pastor.

The father-son conflict represents the head-on clash between the humanistic and the authoritarian consciences. While the battle engenders suffering for all involved, Gertrude, in her innocence, is the victim. Unlike Alissa, and instead of inhibiting the voice of his humanistic conscience, the Pastor tries to adjust to it. Not once does Alissa's love for Jérome distort the voice of her authoritarian self. She may long for a more aggressive Jérome who will vanquish her resistance but, if she is to weaken, it is he who must "force the gate." The Pastor, on the contrary, has unwittingly prepared his victim. He cultivates her innocence, alienates Jacques, then forces the door to her "inner room."

The Pastor's "blind" self-interest, leads to the distortion of conscience which, in turn, leads to the father-son dialogue. Without this dialogue *La Symphonie* would be incomplete. It is the generalization of this father-son conflict, that is the polarization of Protestant-Catholic, conscience-dogma, permissive-authoritarian stances, which illustrates the moral framework within which Gide places his art. Gide blends moral antitheses as artistic counterpoints of white and black, light and dark, good and evil.

Gide's own *Journal* helps to explain the meaning of the father-son dialogue so sketchily developed in *La Symphonie*. In 1913 he wrote that the first duty of a Christian is to be happy. He stressed Christ's "admirable words": "Why do you cry?" These words are the basis for the Pastor's and Gertrude's conversation about happiness. The Pastor will not let Gertrude read St. Paul because he feels that commandments and sin stand in the way of happiness. His subsequent exchange of notes with his son opposes Christ and St. Paul who, in turn, become the proponents of a vast symbolic structure of good and evil. The Pastor, according to Hytier, uses Christ to suit his own instincts,[1] which means that the Pastor has glimpsed the possibilities of a personal morality of love which he is now desperately trying to reconcile with his previous Christianity. He searches the Gospels in vain for commands, threats, and prohibitions. All of these, he concludes, come from St. Paul. On May 3 the Pastor writes that Jacques and those like him "would obtain by compulsion what would readily be granted by love."

> "But, Father," says Jacques, "I too desire the soul's happiness."
>
> "No, my friend, you desire its submission."
>
> "It is in submission that happiness lies."

The polarity between freedom and submission to authority is not only the mold within which Gide's art evolves, it governs the moral implications of this conflict which are at the very heart of the Protestant-Catholic dialogue.

> I am surprised [says Gide] that Protestantism, in rejecting the Church's hierarchies, did not also reject the oppressive teachings of Saint Paul, the dogmatism of his epistles, in order to rely exclusively on the Gospels.[2]

Although the reader may criticize the Pastor for not exposing Gertrude to life's ugliness and contradictions still, Gide seems to be saying, had it not been for the zeal with which Jacques fed her evident disenchantement with the visible world on the dogma of St. Paul, she might have survived the moment of peril. Gertrude, like Alissa, prefers death to life. Both heroines' submission to or guidance by religious authoritarianism destroys them. Gertrude accepts St. Paul's doctrine and, like Jacques, is converted to Catholicism, while Alissa submits to a Calvinistic austerity which, for Gide, is as repugnant as St. Paul's dogma:

> My Christianity [says Gide] comes only from Christ. Between him and me, I see Calvin and St. Paul as two equally evil screens. Ah! if only Protestantism had been able immediately to cast aside St. Paul! But it is to St. Paul and not to Christ that Calvin is specifically related.[3]

Whatever we may think of the Pastor's interpretation of Christ's teachings he construes the Gospels in a way which, essentially, Gide approves. The Pastor's identification of love, joy, freedom, and happiness, deriving from Christ's teachings, are almost identical with statements Gide intersperses throughout his *Journal*.[4]

If this is true, why does the Pastor fail and why is Gide critical of him? I dare say that Gide is critical only of the fact that the Pastor did not go far enough in rejecting the Protestant tradition. Such a rejection would, of course, negate the Pastor's career, separate him from his wife (his son is already in a monastery), and heighten the tragedy of his isolation. Had Gertrude lived and had she been able to love the Pastor's furrowed brow (since she does love his "mind"), the logical conclusion to their pagan idyl would have been a departure, together and "disponible," toward the "eternal city" which attracted Angèle and the naked Meliboeus.

Evil, in addition to the Pastor's inadequacies, subversive as this notion might be (Gide surely intended it this way), emanates from Amélie's austere Protestantism and Jacques' dogmatic Catholicism. But the Pastor's cecity is even greater than Gertrude's. He cannot understand or bring to consciousness the full implications of his love for her which, by its (love's) very nature, must reject Jacques and Amélie.

Consequently, Gide's authorial values, contained within the artistic structure of *La Symphonie,* expose the flaws in the moral position of both father and son. In fact, the book demonstrates that the introspective Protestant minister, who communes directly with God through prayer and who relies on his "conscience" to solve the most delicate emotional problems, will rationalize the nature of his true motives and act as though "blind." For the sake of Gertrude's welfare, and in the name of his "conscience," he will invent reasons to prevent her marriage and he will contrive reasons for keeping Jacques at a distance. He says: "An instinct as sure as conscience warned me that I had to prevent this marriage at all cost" (March 8).

Obviously, the Pastor does not want to lose her. His "good faith" cleverly leads the reader into a web of deceit which, if it was not apparent at first, will explain the nature of Jacques' behavior. Jacques, in reaction to his father's frequent appeals to conscience, rejects an introspective Protestantism which has now become suspect. Since his father uses "conscience" to interfere with the son's love for Gertrude, Protestantism, so the son concludes, must not be reliable. Jacques espouses a "stricter" and "more rigid" discipline which leads him to Catholicism. On May 30, in his journal, the Pastor records his son's criticism: "My father, . . . it is not fitting that I should accuse you, but it is the example of your error that has enlightened me."

Jacques, so sketchily developed throughout most of the book, suddenly becomes an important character—a master dialectician whose opposition is now essential for the denouement. This story, whose first title was *L'Aveugle* (*The Blind One*), and which was to have been about the moral and intellectual development of Gertrude, opens onto terrain already scarred by the diggings of Gide's favorite and perhaps obsessive theme—the conflict between freedom and submission to authority. This conflict was, from the beginning, the domain of the Gidean dialogue. In 1912 he wrote: "Catholicism is inadmissible. Protestantism is intolerable. Yet I feel myself profoundly Christian." [5]

La Symphonie, like Gide's other works, is essentially "critical" in nature. However, since Gide is not the Pastor, even though it is possible to argue similarities, and since as author he does not openly intrude to comment on the narrative, we must look at the irony which allows him to criticize without actually appearing to do so. The Pastor's description of Beethoven's symphony, as narrated in the February 29 entry in his journal, is illuminating. He writes: "Gertrude had remained silent and as though *drowned* [my emphasis] in ecstasy." Gertrude then asks the Pastor if the world he sees is really as beautiful as that scene which the music describes "by the banks of the stream." Beethoven's second movement, "Scene by the Brook," is as Berlioz said, a movement "devoted to contemplation"—the kind one drowns (pleasurably) in.

From the narrative we know that later Gertrude will "try" to drown herself while picking forget-me-nots *by the stream.* Other passages establish an ironic correlative between light and God—an analogy which associates the light of Gertrude's newly acquired vision with suffering and ugliness. The juxtaposition is enough to shatter her illusions about truth and beauty. The world she sees after the operation is, in spite of, or perhaps because of, the Pastor's overprotection, ugly. She finds no correspondence in visual reality to the ineffable harmonies she hears in Beethoven's music.

On February 28 the Pastor writes, "White I nevertheless tried to tell her [Gertrude] is the extreme treble limit where all tones blend, just as black is the darkest base register." And further on: "imagine white as something absolutely pure, as something in which there is no remaining color, but only light; black, on the contrary, as so charged with color, that it becomes totally dark."

The Pastor gives Gertrude the four Gospels, the Psalms,

the Apocalypse, and the three Epistles of St. John to read but not St. Paul. The Pastor teaches her that "God is light, and in him, is no darkness at all." Also that God "is the light of the world." How then will she be able to reconcile the world she has been taught to believe in with the "black" world she sees after her operation? There will be contradictions on every level which Gide announces periodically and thematically throughout the book.

The themes, as we have seen, are structured in musical, visual, and moral terms. Diagrammatically they may be charted as follows:

light	.... dark:	musical tones
white	.... black:	visual correlatives
GERTRUDE		
good	.... evil:	metaphysical tones
the Pastor	...... Jacques:	moral correlatives
(humanistic)	(authoritarian)	

Gertrude, who is physically, morally, and emotionally blind, is trapped in the middle (where the *extremes* meet) of oppositions which are constantly shifting, evolving and, like the sounds of music with which the novel is enveloped, forever flowing one into the other. It is no doubt the "blinding" complexity of a reality which has lost all meaning (surely Gide's intential irony) that causes Gertrude's foot to "slip" into the stream in which a person "may drown pleasurably."

Another allusion, probably as caustic as the *blindness* metaphor that is both physical and moral, actual and symbolic, is the implication that it is God who has led the Pastor astray. Does the Pastor not pray and is it not God who "tells" him to adopt the destitute girl? Is it not after communion with God that he sends Jacques on his hiking trip and thus tampers with Jacques' and Gertrude's nascent love? Later will not the Pastor stress the purity of his own affection for her? "I refused to recognize anything forbidden in my feelings which leaned so passionately toward Gertrude" (25 April). In the name of love and within the permissive aura of Christ's teachings (in contrast to the stern authoritarianism of St. Paul), the Pastor will insist that "there can be no evil in love."

The Pastor's error is not that he loved Gertrude, but that he "mistook" *this* love for the voice of his former Protestant God. On May 21 the Pastor writes: "I am trying to rise above the idea of sin; but sin to me seems intolerable and yet I do not want to abandon Christ. No, in loving Gertrude, I cannot accept sin. . . . not to love her would be to betray her: she needs my love." Or so he thinks. In reality he is the one who needs her love for he admits the possibility that in order to love God he must love Gertrude. At the end of the book and in the throes of a moral crisis Amélie, his wife, will have to pray for him since his heart is "more arid than the desert."

Gertrude's moral and intellectual development has failed because the Pastor has not prepared her to see the world as it is. He has failed for selfish reasons, partly, but also because of a defect in the Protestant "conscience" which Gide is exposing. The Pastor says that it was conscience rather than reason which guided his conduct. But this variation of Pascal's aphorism on the "heart's reasons" being more reasonable than reason suggests that, if the Protestant reliance on conscience (which, Protestants tell us, is man's surest way to commune with himself and God) can lead to the death of a blind girl, the dubious conversion of a son, and the moral crisis of a minister of God, then conscience, or God, or both are not always reliable.

Both Gertrude and Jacques are the victims of the Pastor's "conscience." He looks upon Gertrude as a stray sheep and as a prodigal daughter in need of salvation. But his comparison is erroneous. Gertrude is neither a black sheep nor a prodigal. There is no connection between the sinner who has gone astray and the poor, destitute, pre-adolescent, blind, animal-like creature the Pastor has adopted. He adopts her, as he says, because he senses that not to do so would have been an act of cowardice before

God, but is it not odd that, during the return journey, he should clasp to his breast this small vermin-infested body "without a soul"? The act, or gesture, is so reminiscent of Saul (in Gide's play *Saül*) clasping the devils to himself under his tunic that I see the Pastor unconsciously using Gertrude as an agent in his need for self-fulfillment and in his unconscious revolt against God. But if Saul was in open rebellion the word revolt, for the Pastor, is too strong a term. It is, rather, a distortion of "conscience." The Pastor, like Alissa, speaks with God or thinks he is speaking with Him. But the Pastor's God and Alissa's do not use the same language. Alissa's God leads her away from love toward a premature death, while the Pastor's God leads him toward love. But Gide so skillfully blends the voice of a dutiful God with the voice of a passion-God that the Pastor can no longer distinguish between the two.

If for a moment, we suppose that one or both of these voices is not God's, whose is it? The devil's? If, for the sake of argument and, judging from the consequences, it is the devil, then what assurance is there for the Protestant that his inner voice, his conscience, is indeed the voice of God. This is precisely the Protestant's dilemma because, freed from Church dogma and the absolution of the Vatican, he must rely on his own interiorized vision of God. This dilemma explains the swing of the Pastor's son, Jacques, away from his father's unconscious hypocrisy toward the more authoritarian stance of St. Paul. For Jacques, as perhaps for many, it is a logical jump from a dogmatic St. Paul to Catholicism.

Gidean characters do not, as a rule, converse with Catholics. Gide reserves this role for himself, as his dialogue with Claudel, Jammes, Du Bos, and Massis suggests. Since most of Gide's personages have a Protestant mentality they talk, for the most part, with their consciences, that is, with an interiorized voice of God. Though they may talk with other people, the main dialogue cannot be described as social, at least not until Gide's Catholic "dialogue" becomes a public issue. The dialogue is a religious and moral one to the extent that one of the main speakers is

God or someone who either speaks for or passes for God.

In Gide's allocution at the Vieux-Colombier to celebrate Dostoevsky's centenary in 1921, he stated that the
novel in the Western World "except for a very few exceptions, is concerned solely with relationships among men,
relationships of passion or intellect, family or society relationships, or those of social classes—but never, almost
never, of the individual's relationship with himself or with
God—which here takes precedence over all others." [6]
Though referring to Dostoevsky, Gide might easily have
included himself in the category he was describing.

Gide's books, like Dostoevsky's, describe the battles the
protagonists wage with themselves, with God or with the
devil. "The only drama that really interests me and that I
would like to relate again and again is the dispute of every
individual with whatever prevents him from being authentic, with whatever is opposed to his integrity, to his
integration." [7] This is a moral drama and the obstacle on
which Gide focuses is almost inevitably within one of his
characters. Thus God or the devil, as the voices of conscience with which a character is struggling, are interiorized moral obstacles and, as such, form the basis for the
hero's struggle with himself. Generally speaking, the antagonist is a force leading the hero away from integration.
In his search for authenticity he must come to terms with
himself as well as with the voice of authority whether it be
God (*La Porte étroite*), patriotism (*Philoctète*), or a
father (*Geneviève*). This is one of the levels of the Gidean dialogue, though by no means the only one. The
protagonists' ability or inability to resolve the conflicts
engendered by the contradictory voices emanating from
within themselves manifests the nature of the dialogue
and reveals Gide's preoccupations.

On the narrative level, the Pastor's dialogue with God,
which begins as an interiorized monologue (the Pastor's
journal), evolves into his religious and philosophical dialogue with Jacques. But the religious opposition between
Protestantism and Catholicism and the philosophical opposition between freedom and submission are treated so

cursorily as to be fuzzy in outline and generally misunder-
stood. An awareness of these limitations seems to have
prompted Gide to write the following:

> I shall probably be obliged to write a preface to my
> *Aveugle*—which otherwise will continue to be misread.
> In it I would say: if being a Christian without being a
> Catholic amounts to being a Protestant, then I am a
> Protestant. But I cannot recognize any orthodoxy other
> than the Roman orthodoxy, and if Protestantism, whether
> Calvinist or Lutheran, wanted to impose its own on me, I
> would immediately go to the Roman, as the only one.
> "Protestant orthodoxy"—for me these words have no mean-
> ing. I recognize no *authority*; and if I did, it would be that
> of the Church.[8]

That Gide might actually have written such an abstract
preface to *La Symphonie* indicates, to me at least, the
level on which he felt it had been misinterpreted. In *Si le
grain ne meurt* Gide describes the forces which, had he
not liberated himself from them, might have stifled him
completely. In *La Symphonie* Gertrude is the victim of
moral conflicts not unlike those referred to in *Si le grain
ne meurt*. It is significant that she dies. That Alissa dies, is
also significant. Little Boris in *Les Faux-Monnayeurs* dies.
Gide consistently attacks the moral, social, and traditional
forces which thwart the development of the personality
and inhibit the full blooming of the self. In *La Symphonie
pastorale* he seems to be saying that the possibility of an
idyllic pagan love has been destroyed by Protestant error
and Catholic dogma, two of the ego's most injurious
eagles.

5

The Protestant Eagle

The Protestant eagle is a spirited, multihued, and complex bird—almost a Phoenix—which Gide revived periodically whenever his artistic and moral libertinism called for the compensating force of a Puritan antidote. Alissa's Protestant eagle balances Michel's Nietzschean *aquila* in ways similar to those in which *Les Nourritures terrestres* (1897) offsets *Les Cahiers d'André Walter* (1891). In line with such a parallelism, Gide intended *Numquid et tu . . . ?* (1916–19), before the publication of *Les Nouvelles nourritures* (1935), to provide a countervoice to the persona of *Les Nourritures terrestres*.

In spite of the variety of Protestant eagles, three, not yet scrutinized, are of particular interest to the humanistic-authoritarian dichotomy. The presence (or absence) of such birds can easily be noted in *Les Nourritures terrestres, in Numquid et tu . . . ?*, and in the 1916–18 period of Gide's *Journal*.

Les Nourritures terrestres is a striking contrast to *Les Cahiers d'André Walter*. Rougemont describes *Les Nourritures* as "the will to conspicuously oppose the here-and-now of Don Juan to the angelic above-and-beyond of Tristan." [1] André Walter does violence to the flesh and suppresses desire so that, in death, he might be worthy of Emmanuèle (with God), while the narrative voice of *Les Nourritures* sings the immediate joys of this earth and praises transitory satisfactions with a full-throated Dionysiac fervor. Duration for Tristan, as an extension of the constancy of love in death, opposes the ephemeral realization of Don Juan's desire in the present.

While Gide's values do not coincide exactly with the persona of *Les Nourritures* and not at all with André Walter's, the juxtaposition does offer useful comparisons. Don Juan's pursuit of the instant, his wish to capture and experience the intensity of the present, precisely because for him there is no eternity, is in evident contrast to André Walter's behavior. This antagonism is of mythological proportions and Rougemont's stress on this inherent duality in Western culture seems to me correct.

Another characteristic and supplemental duality in Gide's fiction is traceable, through Christianity, back to Plato's metaphysical theory of two-worldism. While the Sophists, in some cases, were challenging the authority of tradition altogether, Plato made morality a form of control which is imposed from the outside. This moral cleavage, this opposition between death in life and life in death, between the soul and the flesh, between eternity and the moment was adopted by Christian theology and has managed to keep itself in a dominant position to the present day. The Reformation, while it gave more scope to the intelligence and conscience of the individual person, as against the claims of an established church, never really challenged the doctrine that standards and ideals had to be imported from some "outer" world beyond man to which he should remain subservient.

The moral issue this duality raises is whether man is capable of acting for himself, of being inner-directed, or whether, by some inherent flaw in his nature, he is incapable of self-direction and must, therefore, be redeemed by an external force we sometimes call God.

The answer to this issue may depend, in part, on how we interpret the story of Adam's fall. If Adam's disobedience was a sin, then indeed man is incapable of obedience and he must constantly be reminded of God's power, his own weakness, and his fall from grace. If, however, this initial act of disobedience, like Prometheus', is the beginning of knowledge and is an inevitable and necessary step toward man's fulfillment in opposition to God's (the Old Testament God), then the question is whether man is to act for himself or for God.

I am defining God as a force "external to" rather than "within" man, a force which is the source of morality and to whose wisdom and omnipotence man submits either through love, or fear, or both. If man acts for himself and refuses to submit the arbitration of his values to such a God, or His representative the Church, then this man or such men claim that an externally imposed value system is not relevant to the problem at hand precisely because it comes from the outside.

This is the essential argument between humanistic and authoritarian ethics, an argument which probably did not originate with Plato and the Sophists but which certainly was perpetuated by them, was the source of argument during the Reformation and is today the basis for conflicting value systems. What is interesting and significant about much of Gide's work is that protagonists like André Walter, Michel, Alissa, or Ménalque become extreme spokesmen within this ethical and metaphysical conflict. While all these protagonists, and others, represent divergent positions, what binds them together is Gide's preoccupation with freedom.

Jean-Paul Sartre was alluding to this issue when he said: "All French thought of these past thirty years, willing or not, whatever its coordinates might have been elsewhere —Marx, Hegel, Kierkegaard—had to define itself *as well* with reference to Gide." [2] Gide's work, therefore, historically, as well as from a contemporary point of view, stands at the center of a living moral conflict. Klaus Mann, though for different reasons, also places Gide within the "crisis of modern thought."

Gide, who seems to have been perfectly cognizant of his role within this cultural cleavage, constantly emphasized the duality of his own nature as well as the double background of his heredity. In his notorious exchange with Barrès he asks if it is his fault that God elected to make him come to this earth between two stars, the product of two races, two provinces, and two confessions. On November 22, Gide's birthday, the earth shifts from the influence of Scorpio to Sagittarius. Since Gide delighted in stressing every possible conflict in his psyche as well as the duality of his origin, he noted in his *Journal*, and with apparent glee, this astrological shift in the heavens.

The "two races" he refers to are the peasant stock from which he is descended on his father's side, and the well-to-do patrician family of his mother, Madame Juliette Gide, née Rondeaux, from Rouen. The "two provinces" are Normandy, where his maternal clan was rooted, and a barren mountainous zone in the South of France where the paternal side lived. The "two confessions" are the Protestant-Catholic polarity (Protestant on his mother's side, Catholic on his father's) which are such an integral part of his heritage. We know that the values of Gide's youth were dominated, even before the death of his lawyer father, by his mother's Calvinism.

The Protestant-Catholic juxtaposition is relevant because Gide will use it to dramatize the "dialogue." But Gide, though he protests against the dogma and authority of the Catholic Church, is neither a modern Luther nor a latter-day Calvin. He reserved this role for fictional characters like André Walter and Alissa.

While the persona of *Les Nourritures* exalts man, Luther and Calvin stressed man's depravity. *Les Nourritures* stresses the reliability of the human, while Luther and Calvin were convinced that man was powerless to save himself on his own merits. The Reformation did emphasize the need for a direct relationship with God, which the Catholic Church had usurped, but it made man submit to the authority of an invisible God Who insisted, as a precondition for salvation, on a complete submission to His will and the subjugation of the individual. *Les Nourritures*, on the other hand, stresses the immanence of God in nature and, instead of the subordination of the self, the full realization of man's powers. While the Catholic Church, like Protestantism, has always denied that man could find salvation on the strength of his own virtues and merits, St. Augustine and the Catholic Church in general, stressed, in a more positive way than the Reformation, the effect of man's own actions upon his fate.

If we recall the Calvinism on which Gide was nurtured, as well as the vein of Catholicism running through his background, it is easy to comprehend how Gide would be attracted by the latitude of freedom Catholicism seemed to offer for salvation while at the same time we can understand why Gide would stress Protestantism's bypassing of the Church for a direct personal relationship with God. Ultimately, in his search for and exploration of freedom, Gide discards both Protestantism and Catholicism in order to achieve total self-determination.

The freedom Gide talks about is probably best understood in terms of submission to or rejection of authority. He does not suggest, however, that in order to be free man must systematically discard or rebel against all authority. Freedom is a relative concept which theologians and poets from St. Thomas to Robert Frost have sometimes defined as feeling free in the yoke. It was because the yoke was too tight for the African natives exploited by the Compagnie Ferrière that Gide attacked certain practices of "capitalism" in his *Voyage au Congo*. It was because he disliked the rigidity of the Soviet system under Stalin that he wrote *Retour de l'U.R.S.S.*

Les Nourritures terrestres is Gide's song to freedom. It exudes joy because, like a serpent shedding its skin, Gide was wriggling out of a moral system which was in the process of stifling him. His psychosomatic ailments, and his consumption in particular, were obviously the body's reaction to an ethical code which had never been in harmony with his subterranean needs. As a poem to happiness, *Les Nourritures* extolls the virtues of self-discovery which, in turn, are a springboard to new and ever-changing possibilities:

> you will notice that everything that is young is tender; and in how many sheaths is not every bud enclosed! But everything that at first protected the tender germ hinders it as soon as the germinating process is complete; and no growth is possible unless these sheaths burst open, having primarily bound them (p. 297).[3]

The experience of writing *Les Nourritures terrestres* represents the kind of germination Gide has in mind. The tone is an inherent part of the moral growth he is advocat-

ing. Like a seed shedding its protective layers Gide discards the incrustations of his mother's joyless Protestantism. He describes physical joy in reaction to asceticism:
"My emotions flowered in me like a divine revelation" (p.
157).

The actions, thoughts, and feelings of the persona in
Les Nourritures terrestres coincide with the unfolding of a
happy personality and produce a feeling of inner approval,
the kind of "rightness" Fromm speaks of as characteristic
of the humanistic conscience. Gide compares the acts,
thoughts, and feelings, prior to this unfolding, to the
crossing of marshlands (we are reminded of *Paludes* and
the Sargasso Sea in *Le Voyage d'Urien*). This earlier
unfulfilled state produces a feeling of uneasiness and dis-
comfort characteristic of a "guilty" conscience. In *Man
for Himself* Fromm defines the humanistic *conscience* as
"*a re-action of ourselves to ourselves.*" The persona of *Les
Nourritures* compares itself to a sleeping and metamor-
phosing chrysalis: "I let the new being that I would
become form within me" (p. 159).

The rightness of the changes slowly manifesting themselves are expressed as a feeling of plenitude until, with an
actual sense of rebirth, the persona discards books, vestiges
of the past, and tradition. The new being basks in the joy
of every instant and in all the conceivable pleasurable
sensations of life. Gone is a morbid and repressive Calvinism which has been shed with other layers of an outmoded
morality. God is identified with happiness and natural
surroundings, capable of producing a state of euphoria:
"life is the only good" (p. 162). Within the framework of
humanistic ethics the persona of *Les Nourritures* is the
voice of the true self calling us (Nathanël) back to ourselves, "Let my book teach you to be more interested in
yourself than in it,—then more in everything else than in
yourself" (p. 153). The persona stresses the individual
nature of all discovery and the joy of partaking of this
world (not the next): "Nathaniel, I will teach you fervor"
(p. 156).

In Book Two this rage to live and to partake of life

reaches a crescendo which, in his 1927 preface, Gide describes as the exuberance of a convalescent. Nevertheless it is perhaps relevant that a Protestant ethic could make him sick and that, in discovering the world, he had to react against the religious influences of his past. Relevant also is the fact that the tone of *Les Nourritures* is one of unlimited happiness. This feeling of rightness contrasts with André Walter's anguish, punitive measures, and acts of retribution against himself. André Walter's and Alissa's "suicides" are the epitome of self-hatred, that is, the voice of conscience turned against the self, whereas the voice of *Les Nourritures* proclaims only love. There is no greater contrast. What Gide is saying essentially is that freedom from constraint, self-love, and happiness go together in the same way as do subservience to authority (external or internalized), self-hate, and unhappiness.

As an autobiographical poem *Les Nourritures* makes sense alone or read independently of Gide's other works. But the perspective of his revolt and self-discovery adds focus and dimension. *Les Nourritures* should preferably be read against the background of *Les Cahiers d'André Walter, Paludes,* and *Le Voyage d'Urien* which describe the marshlands of moral and intellectual stagnation through which Gide had to pass before discovering his "true" yet latent self.

The Protestant eagle might well have devoured Gide had he not rebelled against the forces working toward his destruction. The writing of *Les Nourritures terrestres* demonstrates that Gide could cultivate the voice of his humanistic conscience and, like his Prometheus, eventually cast off the shackles of religious convention.

Nevertheless, nineteen years after the publication of *Les Nourritures,* Gide's "return" to the Protestant ethic prompted many critics to speak of "moral crisis" and near conversion. But Gide's preoccupation with Scripture between 1916 and 1919 is misleading. During this period he was writing *Numquid et tu . . . ?* or the *Cahier Vert* as it is sometimes referred to. "I ardently hope to write that book of meditations or elevations which will balance the *Nourritures . . .*" wrote Gide in his *Journal* on February 1, 1916. The title is a quotation from John, 7: 52, but, by leaving out the word Galilean, Gide seems to have lent an equivocal meaning to the original quotation. "Are ye also led astray? . . . Art thou also of Galilee?" Because Gide replies to all the possible meanings of these questions, there is an ironic ambiguity in the simplicity of his answers. George Painter feels, as I do, that Catholicism, in particular, is made to feel the recoil of every effort Gide makes toward the purity of the Gospels.[4]

Gide had seventy copies published in Bruges in 1922 (he sent one to Claudel) and then, in 1926, brought it out simultaneously with *Si le grain ne meurt*. Claudel wrote from Tokyo on January 12, 1924 to say that Gide's tenacious concern with faith showed that God was still with him.

> I infer from this moving little book that you now admit the divinity of Christ and have begun to pray. That is something as impressive as the moment when a child first begins to breathe. Your great discovery (and in this you are perfectly right) is that eternal life is not deferred till later but begins here and now, from the very moment that the Kingdom of God is with us, *intra nos*.[5]

If *Si le grain ne meurt* is a physical confession then *Numquid* is admittedly, as O'Brien points out, some kind of spiritual confession. But it is probably not the confession he and many critics seem to think it is.[6] While it does represent Gide's spiritual aspirations and preoccupations, in contrast to *Corydon*'s apology for homosexuality and the senses, Gide's reaching out toward God and the divine in no way resembles the traditional attitudes Claudel had in mind when he praised the book. A particularly revealing entry in Gide's *Journal* of January 30, 1916, just before he began writing *Numquid*, shows that he was addressing Christ and God in a very special way:

> If I had to formulate a credo, I would say: God is not behind us. He is to come. It is not at the beginning, but at

the end of the evolution of beings that he must be sought. He is terminal, not initial. He is the supreme and final point in time toward which all nature tends . . .

.   .   .   .

That is the gate through which I enter into the holy place, that is the series of thoughts leading me back to God, to the Gospels, etc.

This is the same language Gide will use during as well as after his "crisis." In other words, man creates God. God is the vision of an edenic morality, which man projects into the future, a vision to which he then willingly submits and which he actively works to bring about. Gide subscribes to Christ's revolutionary morality because he sees it as structuring the future spiritual evolution of mankind

> it is not so much a matter of believing in the words of Christ because Christ is the Son of God, as of understanding that he is the Son of God because his word is divine and infinitely above everything that art and man's vision offer us.
> This divinity is enough for me.[7]

The Lord Gide invokes is not the Son of God in the traditional sense but divine only by virtue of His superiority to other men. Therefore, Gide's submission to this spiritual ideal is tantamount to an acceptance of himself or, I should say, represents the acceptance of a "spiritual" dimension in himself, in contrast to his sexuality which, as his *Journal* entries reveal, was bothering him a great deal at this time (1916). It is the superiority of Christ's *vision* which, in Gide's eyes, makes him *divine*.

> Lord, I listen to your words not because I was told you were the Son of God; but because your words are more beautiful by far than any human words; that is what tells me you are the Son of God (*Numquid*, p. 588).

The language here seems to me unequivocally clear. Gide subscribes to Christ's teachings not because people say he is the Son of God but because such teachings are the expression of the divine within all men. In no sense is Gide interested in a priori divinity. Christ's greatness — the

virtue which established his divinity—is to have proclaimed that the kingdom of God is within every man and
that it can be attained now rather than in some remote
and distant future.

Gide's insistence that the kingdom of Heaven was
within every man accompanied the conviction that such a
charmed state could be attained now rather than in the
future. In *Numquid*, in Gide's *Journal*, and in his *Dosto-
ievsky*, one of the quotations which recurs most frequently
is man's need to be born again before he can enter into
the Kingdom of God. Gide's warning that we must not
spoil our lives for any end, whatever the goal, placed heavy
emphasis on the present. The words *Et nunc* (which
Claudel so quickly responded to) punctuate his writings
and become part of the title of one of his last books, *Et
nunc manet in te* (1947).

> *Et nunc* . . .
> It is *in eternity* right now that one must live. And it is
> *right now* that one must live in eternity.
> What do I care for eternal life without the awareness at
> every instant of its duration?
> Just as Jesus said: "*I AM the way, the truth,* He says: *I
> am the resurrection and the life.*
> Eternal life is not only to come. It is right now wholly
> present in us; we live it from the moment that we consent
> to die to ourselves, to obtain from ourselves this renuncia-
> tion which permits resurrection in eternity. *He that hateth
> his life in this world shall keep it unto eternal life* (*John*,
> 12: 25 and *Numquid*, p. 591).[8]

Many similar passages in *Numquid* might indeed be
ambivalent, were it not for their transposition, verbatim,
into the Dostoevsky book. "What do I care for eternal life
without the awareness at every instant of its duration?"
(*Dostoïevsky*, p. 177). In elucidating Dostoevsky Gide
quotes approvingly from Mark Rutherford's *Autobiogra-
phy* in which Rutherford says that we must not worry
about the sunshine of the future because today's sun is as
beautiful now as it will ever be. As for the notion of

immortality, says Rutherford, men have been happy without it even during times of disaster and despair. He considers it a folly to sacrifice the possibility of present happiness
in order to guarantee one's future immortality and Gide
concurs.

Gide emphasizes, almost *ad nauseam* that eternity, at-
tainable in the present, is at the heart of Dostoevsky's
Christian morality. *Numquid* reveals that it is also an
essential part of Gide. If *Numquid* balances *Les Nourritures terrestres*, it is not in the sense of being its "spiritual"
opposite, but rather its "spiritual" complement. Gide's
"return" to the Protestant ethic during the 1916–19 period
is, therefore, misleading. It is less a return than a reshap-
ing of an ethic designed to give it greater scope and
amplitude. It is, like Gide's prodigal, a subversive return.
Numquid is a disappointing eagle and, contrary to some
expectations, it must have remained scrawny. Surprisingly,
it is in Gide's *Journal* of this period that we find an eagle
plump enough to have caused him some anguish.

Gide's *Journal*, which he kept sporadically from 1889 vir-
tually to the year of his death, in 1951, is an interesting
blend of reflection, commentary, confession, and anecdo-
tal material. No phase of its composition is as revealing of
the "dialogue" and preoccupation with "eagles," specifically Protestant, as a two-year period running approximately from January 1916 to December 1917.

These two years coincide with the writing of *Numquid
et tu . . . ?* and belong to a period of "crisis" in Gide's life
which was caused, in part, by the trauma of the war years.
The First World War was responsible for a number of
conversions including those of Charles Du Bos and
Ghéon. We cannot say accurately, in Gide's case, whether
it was empathy, or a sense of responsibility to the Belgian
war refugees, and the suffering of others which their very
presence implied, that precipitated his "crisis" (since during this time he was helping at the Foyer Franco-Belge).
In 1929 Gide commented retrospectively:

I would not swear that at a certain period of my life I was
not very close to being converted. Thank God, a few
converts among my friends straightened me out. Neither
Jammes, nor Claudel, nor Ghéon, nor Charlie Du Bos will
ever know how much I profited from their example. I
retierate this to myself as I read through the pages of
Charlie's journal, that monument of immodesty and unconscious self-indulgence.[9]

The fact is that certain latent religious preoccupations
became manifest and dominated his feeling and his thinking at this time. Of interest, of course, is that Gide's new
spiritual dialogue was comparable to the moral dialogue of
his fictional characters: the dialogue between self and God
or God's representatives in "conscience." Consequently,
these two years of Gide's *Journal* read very much like a
novel. The language, the themes, and the conflict come
from the "dialogue of opposites" and serve, once again, to
dramatize his life as well as his art.

While engaged in dialogue with his Catholic opponents, and while having made the dialogue of opposing
values one of the themes of his work, Gide also used the
dialogue to dramatize his opposition to his mother as well
as to emphasize the contrast between Madeleine and himself, the "marriage of heaven and hell," as he so frequently
called it.

During 1916 and 1917 this continuing dialogue between
the authoritarian and the humanistic ethic was to be
renewed with an intensity Gide had not experienced since
his struggle for emancipation from his mother's authority
before 1893 was climaxed with the writing of *Les Nourritures terrestres*. The war seems to have precipitated guilt
feelings and apparently opened a few psychic scars left
over from his Puritan childhood: "The cannon's echo
again makes the ground quake, . . . I feel from the outside as well as within me an immense disorder" (15 June
1916). Commenting on the war and those who, including
himself, assumed a personal sense of guilt in reaction to it
Gide wrote, "Today they blame the war; but the evil had
deeper roots" (18 December 1917). This observation

echoes Racine's Phèdre and suggests, in Gide's case, that certain feelings, triggered by the war, have revived a notion of sin in keeping with the early teachings of his mother's Puritanism: "the evil is so profound and deep-rooted, has such impetus, that it upsets all the attention I give it." [10]

"I have no less trouble in reviving within me the idea of sin than I had in extenuating it earlier," wrote Gide on January 28, 1916. When we recall the role *Les Nourritures terrestres* played in exorcising the past we may ask why Gide was trying to restore a state of mind which, for so many years, he had struggled to overcome. The reasons, I suspect, represent a triple blend of genuine guilt brought on by the war, but mixed with curiosity, since Gide was constantly using his psyche as an experimental battleground for opposing values.[11] In 1924 he wrote: "I can say that it is not in myself that I was interested, but in the conflict of certain ideas played out in the theater of my soul where my function was less that of actor than of spectator or witness" (19 March).

Lest we forget the extreme identification Gide underwent in creating his fictional characters, let me quote a 1927, February 8 extract from his *Journal*:

> Nothing is accomplished unless, in this character I am assuming, I have not been truly able to become him, to the point of deceiving myself, and to depersonalize myself in him to the point of being accused of never having known how to portray anyone but myself—however different from each other may be Saul, Candaules, Lafcadio, the Pastor of my *Symphony*, or La Pérouse or Armand. It is returning to myself, that embarrasses me, for, in truth, I no longer fully know who I am; or, if you prefer: I never *am*; I become.

Is it possible that Gide had a novel in mind which never materialized, or was he trying to stress the living fictional affinities between the novel in general and his *Journal*? Probably both since on January 24, 1916, he wrote: "I imagine a novel whose subject would be the enlightenment of this phrase: *'The weight of my sins drags me down.'* " So instead of a novel in which the weight of the hero's sins pulls him down we have a fictionalized biography in which the weight of Gide's role-playing, like the extreme identification with his fictional characters, influences his feelings.

While this "crisis" *seems* sincere enough, Gide retains a certain objectivity and even detachment. How otherwise explain the simultaneous writing of a work as opposite in nature as *Corydon?* Moreover, if it is "by his contradictions that a being interests us and gives evidence of his sincerity" (*Journal,* 29 October 1922), then this further manifestation of what Gide calls the "cohabitation of extremes" is not so much an example of insincerity as it is a revelation of his inherent duality.

> I have never been able to renounce anything; and protecting in me both the best and the worst, it is as a man drawn and quartered that I have lived. But how can it be explained that this cohabitation of extremes in me did not bring so much worry and suffering upon me as the pathetic intensification of the sense of existence, of life? The most opposite tendencies have never succeeded in making a tormented being out of me; but perplexed instead—for torment accompanies a state one wants to get out of, and I had no wish to escape whatever brought into play all the potentialities of my being; that *state of dialogue* which for so many others is almost intolerable became necessary for me. Also because, for those others, it can only inhibit action, whereas for me, on the contrary, far from leading to sterility, it facilitated the work of art and immediately preceded creation, resulting in equilibrium and harmony.[12]

If the cultivation of this duality—the willingness to explore the contradictory dimensions of one's being—is, in part, what Gide calls "sincerity," then the cohabitation of extremes is not a contradiction, but the expression of a fundamental reality. The idea that Gide is trying to restore in himself the notion of sin suggests that he is on the verge of fattening another eagle. That he can make the process look authentic, *be* authentic, is a remarkable example of life imitating art. "I am seeking to organize the struggle . . . What patience and ruse it would take!" (25 January 1916).

Certain *Journal* entries during 1916 and 1917 are the record of this struggle, of this biographical fiction. Gide describes the need to re-educate himself, to fight sexual curiosity, and to resist the imperious lure of some faces for which, he says, he would abandon everything. He even wonders if he will succeed without help, though he rejects Catholicism as any kind of viable solution to his dilemma. He describes a feeling of helplessness in the face of temptation, and wonders at times if he is not crazy (is Gide alluding to the admonishment by Francis Jammes that unless he is converted he will go mad?).

To facilitate the reintegration of sin within himself Gide tries reading Bossuet. But he is not inspired by the first two "élévations" which, far from persuading him, only upset him more.

> No, it is not through *that gate* [my italics] that I can enter; there is no gate for me in that direction. I can play dumb; I have tried it; but not for long, and soon I leap up indignantly against this blasphemous comedy which my being strives to play out. If the Church requires that of me, it is because God remains above the Church. I can believe in God, have faith in God, love God, and my whole heart leans me in that direction. I can submit my mind to my heart. But, for pity's sake, do not look for proofs or reasons (29 January 1916).

Gide's rejection of Bossuet implies a Protestant rather than a Catholic approach to the relationship between man and God. No doubt Pascal's Jansenism appealed to whatever residue of Calvinist determinism was still left in Gide since he found reading Pascal more palatable than Bossuet. As a result Gide soon managed to impose daily meditation on himself, once in the morning and once at night.

In typically Protestant fashion Gide preferred a kind of religious solipsism. The fact that he found no gate open for him in Bossuet reminds us that Gide's method, like

Alissa's, is personal and solitary. Even at the height of his religious fervor he will not follow Claudel's or Jammes' advice that he seek the help of a priest.

Gide compared the conflict between his spirit and his flesh, between heaven and hell, to the struggle going on in the trenches where there was no glory but only small and minor victories. But giving in to temptation was for him like a total and sudden defeat. Gide's struggle between masturbation and continence raised the specter of his youth: should he accept pleasurable sensations or, on the contrary, as his Calvinist upbringing had taught him, should he fight them and, in reprisal, mortify the flesh, like Lafcadio who jabs his thigh with the tip of a pen-knife.

Gide's "unhappiness" during this period will provide an effective contrast to the "happiness" that will immediately follow his return to "normal" around 1918. The point of departure for this biographical fiction, reminiscent of Rimbaud's derangement of the senses, is Gide's struggle against temptation. "It takes determination, but even more, patience. Nothing is less romantic, nothing is more tiresome at times than the minute detail of this moral hygiene" (11 February 1916).

The 1916–18 *Journal*, is an intimate picture of Gide's struggle to resolve or, more appropriately, expose the voices of the two consciences warring for supremacy within him. He has at last become, as his readers always suspected he was, the main character of his fiction. During this period, unlike the previous ones, Gide seems or pretends to identify sexuality and pleasure with the devil and sin. The struggle, typically, is polarized between God and the devil, between good and evil, except that this time Gide has not reversed the meaning of his terms and the traditional Christian framework remains intact.

I shall make no attempt to reconcile differences, if there are any during these two years, between the Gide who emerges from the pages of the *Journal* and the Gide his friends might have known during that time. Gide's *Journal* is, among other things, a very special portrait of the

man, a portrait he himself wished to legate to posterity.
The important thing is that we capture the image Gide
wished to communicate rather than the actual image people might have had of him during that period. Such an
approach also resolves the accusation of insincerity leveled
at him by critics who insist that the facts of his life and his
Journal must necessarily coincide.

The reader will remember my previous reference to St.
Francis of Assisi's "illness" and his refusal to listen to
what he called the "voice of the devil." Now that Gide is
forcing an ascetic role upon himself, he describes as follows his own encounters with the fallen angel:

> And the Evil One is always ready to whisper in my ear:
> "This is all a comedy that you are playing to deceive
> yourself. With the first breath of spring, you will go over to
> the enemy entirely. The enemy? What do you mean by
> enemy? You have no other enemy than your own fatigue. If
> it were more open, your sin would be glorious. Therefore be
> frank, and admit that if you speak here of sin, it is because
> the dramatic effect is convenient for you and helps you to
> recover an agility you felt was being jeopardized, the free
> control of flesh and mind. Today you take your physi-
> cal weariness for moral decay; soon, when you are cured,
> you will blush for having believed it necessary to resort to
> such means in order to cure yourself:" Meanwhile, I am
> still ill—and will remain ill as long as I listen to this voice
> (11 February 1916).

The dramatization is obvious. For the moment, at least,
Satan speaks for the humanistic conscience while Gide
embodies the authoritarian. By the end of 1917 the roles
will be, once again, reversed. From then on the voice of
Satan will definitely be the authoritarian conscience.
Satan will be identified with the voice of the dictatorial
whether Protestant ethic, Catholic Church, or Communist state.

In the meantime, the ascetic voice is God's and it is this
commanding voice, left over from Gide's childhood,
which tells him he is sick and will remain sick as long as
he listens to the devil. This is the meaning of Gide's

playacting. In any case, his self-dramatization seems to be working since he has now adopted the moral view of the authoritarian conscience: "I ask God humbly this morning: My Lord, sustain me, guide me, protect me throughout this day" (4 April 1916).

Gide tells us that insomnia frequently accompanies the intellectual ferment of his creative process. The disturbance that is really interesting, however, is not so much the insomnia as Gide's hostility to himself.

> A disgust, an atrocious self-hatred sours all my thoughts from the moment I awake. The carefully wrought hostility with which I spy on every movement of my being makes me writhe. Faults or virtues, I no longer possess anything natural. Everything that my being recalls to me horrifies me (20 September 1916).

He cannot, since he is torn by the voices of both consciences, be faithful to either.

It is difficult to explain Gide's return to a religious dilemma which he had apparently solved to his satisfaction as early as 1893. If Gide's 1916 "crisis" represents the resurgence of an authoritarian conscience which he had buried in North Africa but never killed, then we can understand how the war trauma might actually have been the cause of a regression to an earlier state of mind. While Gide is demonstrating how regression works he seems to function within the framework of artistic artifice.

Not only does Gide describe the physical symptoms of the struggle (neurasthenia, restlessness, sleepiness in the daytime, insomnia at night, headaches, fatigue, and general malaise), but on October 15, 1916 his self-disgust has become a state of despair verging on suicide and madness.

His struggle is characterized by long empty days during which he feels submerged in sadness. He experiences such a loss of energy and desire that he concludes finally: "Don't you realize that you are speaking to a dead man?" (Monday, end of September 1916).[13] There is irony here, since in *Numquid* Gide quotes the Bible to the effect that man must lose his life in order to gain it. But if the former self must die before the new man may bask in divine grace, Gide will, in the end, refuse the kind of submission which denies not only his spontaneity but also his *élan vital*.

In addition to irony Gide creates analogies between the wintry landscapes of his estate and the state of his emotional freeze. The weather, the dreary skies, and the arrested growth of trees and plants project an image of bleak atrophy. By establishing the connection between an inner and outer *paysage* Gide provides an oblique commentary on the meaning of his spiritual turmoil and physical distress. He blames the cold wind and the humidity for a black excrescence which has stunted most of the trees. But he takes pleasure in pruning them with his gardener Edmond—a process which, for Gide the botanist and novelist, is always associated with a subsequent flowering of particular vigor. Small wonder that he should eagerly anticipate the new spring growth (19 March 1916). One month later he makes a particularly illuminating entry in his *Journal*:

> Whence comes the *sap's* strange *retreat*, to which my mind is subject so often, and which leaves it laden with dead brushwood? And then you think: a little sap and again this awful dry wood will be covered with leaves and flowers . . . But, dry, it is awful—destined for the fire, done with (18 April 1916).

Why does Gide stress the spiritual withdrawal of sap and compare his psyche to dead wood? What are the cold wintry blasts which have atrophied his soul and produced a state of mind verging on madness and despair? This is hardly the comforting language one would expect from a return to religious faith. As long as his "experiment" lasts he can write only of physical malaise and ennui. Nor does the apparent calm of *Numquid* contradict the *Journal*. *Numquid*, as we have seen, is a deceptive document which appears to voice subservience to a traditional Christian God but which, in reality, it does not. Both the *Journal* and *Numquid* attack the internalized voice of religious authority which Gide finds as antipathetic as the more obvious external authority of Catholicism.

Throughout most of the two "crisis" years Gide's spiritual landscape is bleak, dreary, and cold.

> Fatigue and constant headaches. This morning, when I woke up, it was drizzling. The sky is all gray, with no more blue or sunrays than there is in my thought (Friday, end of September 1916).[14]

Bad weather and diseased trees are the objective correlatives of Gide's illness. A quotation from *Les Nourritures terrestres* might illustrate even further the particular association in Gide's mind between trees and winter landscape:

> From the highest of their high branches, the freed eucalyptuses were shedding their old bark—it was hanging, a worn-out covering, like clothing you take off in the sun, like my old morality good only for the wintertime (Pléiade, p. 180).

The distinction between a morality for winter and another for the springtime—the kind of growth or absence of growth associated with each—leaves little doubt as to Gide's preference.

As long as Gide is the victim of ennui the skies are gray and the weather oppressive. Conversely, he will choose good weather and clear skies to signal his "recovery"—the advent of a state of joy and fervor which this religious period had banished. "Today the weather is glorious. My inner sky is even more splendid; an immense joy thaws and elates me" (1 October 1917). By the end of 1917, as this quotation suggests, the "crisis" has ended.

These years of "crisis," covering 1916 and 1917, are definitely Gide's final catharsis. By casting off the wintry stunted landscape of his soul Gide was, in essence, casting off the vestiges of an austere Puritanism which, in *Si le grain ne meurt*, he compares to the intrusion, into a landscape, of Swiss pine trees.[15] My own feeling, however, is that this "crisis" is more contrived than real. There is a shade of doubt, nevertheless, which adds even greater verisimilitude to the eagle this Protestant-Prometheus is killing.

Gide has exorcized his "demon," killed the Protestant eagle and, once again, presented us with an artist's version of the struggle. Madeleine's burning of his letters, during his escapade in England, seems to be, in this context, an irony almost beyond comprehension, yet terribly appropriate, since she was burning a spiritual self of Gide's which he himself had so obviously discarded.

The resolution of the conflict between the two ethics was not to be accomplished without a final and demonstrable spasm, since the *Journal* entry for September 19, 1916 represents an ambivalent point of view.

> Yesterday, an abominable relapse. The storm raged all night. This morning it is hailing heavily. I get up, my head and heart heavy and empty: full of the entire weight of hell . . . I am the drowning man who is losing heart, and now struggles only weakly. . . .
>
> If I could only relate this drama; depict Satan, after he has taken possession of someone, using that person, affecting others through him.

In portraying the drama between his sensual self and his ascetic self Gide remains detached artistically while becoming involved emotionally. Whenever his sexuality is equated with the devil it is the authoritarian self which holds sway and, naturally, vice versa whenever his asceticism is less dominant. In dramatizing the conflict, which with ironic modesty he says he wishes he could narrate, he anticipates the outcome (the defeat of asceticism) from the beginning. Yet, as spokesman for the authoritarian voice, Gide compares himself to the woman in the Bible who was possessed by the devil for eighteen years (10 March 1917). If vanquishing the devil produces a state of morose Calvinism then we are not surprised that Gide terminates his "experiment" and returns to the joyous enthusiasm of his free, uninhibited self.

I have lived all the time lately (and, altogether, since May 5) in a daze of happiness; whence the long empty space in this notebook. It reflects only my clouds (22 October 1917).

Three days later Gide says he has never been happier nor has the taste of life been more delicious. And the following month he writes:

My joy has something untamed, savage in it, broken off from all decency, all law. Through it I return to the stammering of childhood, for it presents only novelty to my mind. I need to invent everything, words and gestures; nothing from the past satisfies my love any more. Every thing in me is flowering, loosening; my heart beats; a superabundance of life rises to my throat like a sob. I no longer know anything; it is a vehemence without memories and without wrinkles (30 November 1917).

On December 15, 1917, Gide notes that he has not experienced a comparable state of lyricism since writing *Les Nourritures.*

By the end of December 1917 Gide has recovered entirely from his "illness" and is hard at work on *Corydon*, a work of the devil as far as his Protestant eagle is concerned. The Protestant eagle, like Prometheus' chains, was ankylosing him. Gide stretches, removes the fetters of an inhibiting ethic, and, like Meliboeus, walks down the boulevard, not toward Rome, but with Marc toward London.

Rise, naked and valiant; split open your wrappings; thrust aside the supports; to grow straight you need nothing now but the surge of your sap and the call of the sun.[16]

6

The Catholic Dialogue

On April 3, 1952, Gide's works were put on the Vatican *Index* by official decree of Pope Pius XII. Soon thereafter, on June 1, 1952, *L'Osservatore Romano* published an article justifying the condemnation. Gide was defined as a subversive whose false values and blasphemous statements were shocking to honest, devout, and good-thinking people. His last books were described as anti-Catholic, anti-Christian, anti-Church, and anti-God.

> No one has ever spoken of responsibility so often, nor with an irresponsibility so pronounced that it seemed morbid and incurable. We remain stupefied in seeing to what extent, in his last pages, right up to the very end, he persists in his customary obscenity.[1]

It is perhaps surprising that the Church, unlike many of Gide's critics, waited until his death to condemn him. It did have reason to hope for an ultimate return to faith, however, in view of Claudel's success in converting so many of Gide's friends. Since Gide was also the target of Claudel's proselytising, the Church, perhaps anticipating the success of such efforts, waited until the last possible moment before denouncing him officially. On his deathbed, according to Jean Delay, Gide murmured that it was always "The struggle between what is reasonable and what is not." These final words, while seemingly ambiguous, seem to have dimmed the remnants of lingering hope for those who would have liked to see him take the last sacraments.

A few days after his death there was some hilarity in Paris over a telegram received by Mauriac, signed André Gide. It read: "There is no hell. You can go on a spree. Inform Claudel." [2] This message was the concluding installment to a Catholic "dialogue" which began around 1895 with Francis Jammes, was continued after 1905 by Claudel, and was to be picked up alternately and intermittently by Charles Du Bos, Jacques Maritain, Henri Massis, Jacques Rivière, Henri Béraud, François Mauriac, Jacques Lévy, and Julian Green, to name only ten of the Catholics who tried to influence Gide's thinking. The seriousness of the effort was not without its comic moments, as the last telegam indicates. Earlier, Gide had stated that Claudel was a man who thought one could go to heaven in a Pullman. Claudel's answer had been that Gide was going to hell in the subway.[3]

While Gide himself talked of conversion around 1905 and 1916, he quickly recovered from both "religious crises" and from then until his death, his attitude toward religion in general, and Catholicism in particular, was marked by an increasing hostility and impatience. In 1926 he noted that pious Catholics indulge in such absurd excesses as to inhibit common sense in others and thereby invite rebellion and blasphemy (*Journal*, 14 July 1926). Nevertheless Gide corresponded extensively with Jammes and Claudel, not really to exorcise a Catholic eagle, since he never had one, but to demonstrate the foolish excesses of pious proselytising. By 1937, however, he had decided to end the dialogue:

> No discussion with them is possible. We bear a respect to them, their convictions, and their faith which they are obligated, in the name of their faith, not to bear toward us. Their self-assurance is their strength; they are content to see only arrogance in our resistance, only weakness in our circumspection. What, for us, is an indispensable virtue: intellectual integrity, is in their eyes merely an obstacle to believing which must be surmounted.[4]

When we consider the fact that, at varying times, Gide compared Catholicism to a gangrene and to Hitlerism and that he frequently mocked its excesses, it is not surprising that the article in *L'Osservatore Romano* was as virulent as it was. On the other hand since Gide, during his lifetime, was subject to constant attack by Massis, Béraud and others like them, for the alleged immorality of his writings, we can expect and certainly detect in his later years an estrangement from those who, in the name of Church dogma, proclaimed a higher moral self-righteousness. What the Vatican was objecting to, however, was not merely Gide's attack on its authority; it accused him also of perverting the meaning of God and of deifying Satan. Gide was, in effect, subverting the roots of an authoritarian doctrine which, he believed, was responsible for the proliferation of counterfeit values.

> Smiling submissiveness is no longer my strong point at all. If I am not more insistent it is because I believe that insinuation is more effective. People resist what shocks them and in turn they protest. It is a matter of persuasion, and I believe that it can be achieved by asking the other person to reflect rather than by meeting him head on (*Journal*, 2 August 1931).

Counterfeit values were, in turn, the source of inauthentic beings. *Les Faux-Monnayeurs* and its sequels *L'Ecole des femmes, Robert,* and *Geneviève* concern themselves with this problem. "Religion and the family are the two worst enemies of progress" (*Journal*, 27 July 1931). Gide was careful, however, not to single out any particular family. Rather, he spoke of families in general ("Families, I hate you!") since he saw bad faith (to use Sartre's expression) being defended in the name of honor and family tradition.

Gide was looking for a rational, humane, self-directed man. Now that he had come to believe in "progress" (the possibility of man's perfectibility), in contrast to his "Promethean" days, he felt that this concept was being inhibited by irrational, intolerant, other-directed men. It was inevitable that God and then the family, the two bastions of authority, should come under his attack.

It strikes me as monstruous that man should need the idea of God in order to feel steady on earth; that he should be forced to accept absurdities in order to construct anything solid; that he should recognize himself incapable of demanding of himself what religious convictions obtained from him artificially, so that he lets everything go to nought as soon as his heaven is emptied (*Journal*, 20 October 1927).

According to Gide, subservience to authority (God, Church, State, or family) puts the will to sleep and inhibits effort. "Faith moves mountains; yes: mountains of absurdities." [5]

The Church, quite understandably, attacked Gide for such "blasphemy." Nevertheless, in *Numquid*, in his *Dostoïevsky*, and in *Les Nouvelles nourritures* Gide insisted repeatedly that man's salvation *on earth* could not wait for faith or for an afterlife. Since he did not believe in an afterlife, the emphasis, inevitably, was on the present (*Journal*, 11 January 1943). Nor did Gide believe in the separation of the body and the soul (*Journal*, 15 May 1949). The death of one, he said, implied the disappearance of the other. So it was quite logical that on his deathbed Gide should have continued to protest against the "unreasonable."

While, generally speaking, he advocated a state of complete atheism it was not because he wished free license for himself or for others. His polemic with Barrès on the question of "déracinement" was a decisive blow to laziness. In fact, Gide's emphasis on effort, as the concomitant for self-development, argued against the exclusive indulgence of the senses. Gide wanted man, as if he were a tree, to mature as a tree, and not as a bush. Authority, he felt, inhibited the natural process of development, whereas self-directed constraint worked in favor of more vigorous and more beautiful growth.

Nor was it a question in Gide's mind of mere random growth as much as the encouragement of a specific human potential which needed care and pruning in order to reach maximum height. Gide identified such fulfillment with creative self-discipline. Only the sustained self-discipline of the inner-directed man, he argued, could effect the kind of change in the self and in human relationships which could be defined as "progress." His idea of progress was based on an effort at self-creation, in defiance of all a priori systems.

> But cannot man learn to demand of himself, through virtue, what he thinks is demanded by God? He must nevertheless manage to; at least some must, to start with; otherwise the game would be up. This strange game that we are playing on earth (unwittingly, unknowingly, and often unwillingly) will be won only if the idea of God, as it recedes, yields to virtue; only if man's virtue and dignity supersedes and supplants God. God has ceased to exist except by virtue of man. *Et eritis sicut dei.* (It is thus that I wish to understand that old word of the Tempter—who, like God, exists only in our minds—and to see in this offer, which we have been told is fallacious, a possibility of salvation.) [6]

Gide indicated that man can save himself by eliminating God as an authorial figurehead. God is then redefined as virtue which is equated with the kind of achievement that brings out the best in man. Consequently God is always in the process of becoming. *He* is in the future and *His* existence is entirely dependent on man: *"man is responsible for God"* (*Journal*, 10 April 1942).

> From the moment that I understood that God was not yet, but was becoming, and that he depended on each one of us for his becoming, my own moral sense was restored. No impiety, no presumption in this thought; for I was convinced that God was achieved only by man and through man at the same time; nevertheless, if man led to God, creation, in order to lead to man, started from God; so that the divine could be found at both ends, at the start and at the point of arrival, and that the start was there in order to take man to God. This double-valved thought reassured me and I was no longer willing to dissociate one from the other: God creating man in order to be created by him; God the end of man; chaos raised up by God to man's

level, and then man raising himself up to God's level. To admit only one of them: what fear, what obligation! To admit only the other: what conceit! It was no longer a matter of obeying God, but of making him come alive, of falling in love with him, of demanding him for oneself out of love and by getting him through virtue (*Journal*, 3–7 June 1942).

It is quite clear, according to Gide, that man (by his own efforts, that is by his virtue), is capable of creating an ideal morality named God. It is less clear, and Gide, no doubt, purposely meant his idea of a creation which began with God to be ambiguous. This second definition, in the natural order of things, would have to precede the first, since God is behind a creation which engenders man, who then in turn creates God. But the two Gods are not the same. The first God, a throwback perhaps to Voltaire's deism, seems to be a naturalistic one whom Gide identifies with the Universe and its creative force—God, the clock-maker, who sets the world in motion. This motion, which Gide seems to define as evolution finally created a being called man. The second God is created by man. Man projects a certain moral perfectibility onto the screen of future history, calls it God, and then strives to fulfill this vision of an ideal world.

If we interpret the "death of God" which, ever since Nietzsche first announced it, has been gaining popularity, as meaning that there will be no future significant biological changes (evolution) in man, then in order to live again, God, envisioned as a process of moral human perfectibility, has to be recreated anew from within man. Biologists like Julian Huxley define this process as the future social evolution of man. Gide would have concurred. Hence his fear of stasis and his emphasis on the desirability of change. To remain immobilized leads to moral and spiritual atrophy and, eventually, to the tyranny of dogma.[7]

Gide's hatred of spiritual and physical tyranny is sufficient to explain his rejection of Catholicism and, ultimately, of communism as well. While François Mauriac, as an enlightened Catholic, tried to impress on Gide the fact that not all of the faithful were as reactionary as Claudel or Henry Massis, Gide preferred to define and attack the particular brand of Catholicism as advocated by its least liberal representatives. The uncompromising rigidity of the reactionary Catholic right was a better bouncing board for Gide's moral and artistic purposes since he could better define himself in opposition to it. Nonetheless it is significant that the tone of the Vatican condemnation belongs to this reactionary right. The fact that the Vatican attacked Gide for his atheism is quite understandable. That it should label him obscene and irresponsible confirms his and their irreconcilable opposition of values.[8]

Gide wanted to make man responsible to himself rather than to the doctrine of a transcendent God, since this is the ultimate moral responsibility of the self-directed man.

> My heredity, then my Protestant formation inclined my mind almost exclusively toward moral problems. In those earlier times, I had not yet understood that the duties toward God and those toward oneself could be the same. Now, I have a great tendency to confuse them too completely. I remain demanding; much more toward myself than toward others; but I no longer believe that it is someone other than myself, some power superior to me, and independent of me, which does the demanding.[9]

Since Gide refuses to recognize an allegiance to an authority outside of himself, he equates God with the voice of the humanistic conscience. While Gide can be accused of deifying man, his emphasis on man's moral responsibility to others as well as to himself is neither immoral nor irresponsible.

As a moralist in the highest sense of the French tradition Gide was advocating a new morality which preceded, yet now in retrospect, shows striking parallels with the thought of Sartre, Erich Fromm, and the psychologist Carl Rogers.[10] While Sartre's phenomenology does not provide for the distinctions I have been making between the *voices* of "conscience," his emphasis on choice, bad faith and the need for authenticity of being are direct extensions of Gide's thought. In fact, Gide is an existentialist before the hour, since he is, in essence, asking man to reinvent and to recreate himself anew whenever a choice is to be made. Since Gide refused the ready-made answers of a priori moral systems, he was asking man to choose not in the name of the past, or of tradition, or of the family, or of religion, but to evaluate every new situation freshly and spontaneously before determining a course of action. Such an approach to solving problems would, he argued, eliminate counterfeit values and replace them with the genuine currency of the authentic self.

I have already used Erich Fromm's definitions for the humanistic and the authoritarian conscience. As for Carl Rogers, his emphasis on "client-centered" therapy and "non-directive" counseling are predicated on the assumption that the solution to a problem will be more effective, more vital, and more lasting if discovered for himself by the individual, rather than imposed or even suggested from without by a more "capable" authority. John Dewey's system of progressive education is based, is it not, on the assumption that the individual is more able to determine his own needs than someone else.

But this ability of man for self-determination assumes a "healthy" individual without the self-destructive tendencies that often accompany the traumas of living. Gide does not believe (within the context of man and his environment), like Rousseau, that man is inevitably good or like Dewey, that the child necessarily chooses what is best for him. He believes in man's potential for good based on the fulfillment of certain preconditions (rejection of dogma, search for the authentic self, and so forth). His books, demonstrating how characters as different as Michel and Alissa who have listened to their inner selves, have failed, make us more aware of certain inevitable dangers along the way. His fiction unveils the pitfalls of "conscience." Gide is suggesting that it is not easy for man to progress but that this creation of God is perhaps what human destiny is all about. One can disagree with such a view of man and the world but to label it "irresponsible" and "old hat" represents a singularly misinformed point of view. Gide's emphasis on a permissive diversity is clearly an inherent part of twentieth-century thought.

Furthermore, Gide draws attention to responsibility and the moral dimension which lends unity to his books by making his life and his *Journal* an integral part of the artistic process. His often repeated assertion that he was going to write a book, to be called *Le Christ contre le christianisme,* which he never did write, suggests the scope of his interest and the orientation of his thought. Such a separate book was not really necessary, since Gide's works and his life embody all the ideas he might have written into it. While we must not carry the analogy too far, there is a certain perverse resemblance, which Gide himself obliquely cultivated, between Christ's challenge to an established status quo and Gide's attack on social and family tradition. It was Gide's contention that the Church for Catholics, and a certain morose Calvinism for Protestants, have sapped, distorted, and institutionalized the vitality of Christ's thought. The role of Gide's proposed book would have been to bring man back to the roots of an inner, self-directed and, therefore, vital and responsible morality. In 1931 he wrote: "No progress is possible for humanity unless it shakes off the yoke of authority and tradition" (*Journal,* 17 March 1931).

In 1893 he wrote that his efforts of that year were directed toward the process of shedding the straitjacket of religion which was inhibiting his development.[11] Gide seems to have sensed, however, that while he had to discard the incrustations of an official morality in order to affirm his own personality, there were elements in "enemy" doctrine which could still edify and fortify him in the struggle against it.

This typically Gidean method of affirming and strengthening his personality, in opposition to alien principles, is the backbone of his artistic dialogue. The eagle-Prometheus metaphor, and the "Catholic dialogue," as a further fattening of eagles, are an extension of his moral and aesthetic preoccupations. This "aviculture" of his begins approximately in 1893, the year he experienced the reversal of values which was not only to reorient his life, but was to furnish the subject matter of his writings for many years to come.

Gide's correspondence with Claudel and Jammes, while it does not read as though it were "trumped up," does appear now to have been directed by the same moral-aesthetic touch that guided the duality of his fiction. Claudel and Jammes, as the spokesmen for an orthodox Catholicism, are cast in the role of unyielding absolutists.

Gide apparently cultivated these Catholic "opponents" in the same way he nourished the "buds of his fiction." He managed, thereby, to structure a correspondence in which the confrontation of moral values resembles the ethical antitheses in his work. In *Si le grain ne meurt* he commented retrospectively:

> Until the present I had accepted Christ's code of morals or at least a certain puritanism which I had been taught as being Christ's code of morals. In order to force myself to submit to it, I had brought about a profound upheaval of my whole being (Pléiade, p. 550).

Since the morality of his youth had served only to stifle and sicken him, Gide embarked on a course of action which would systematically rid him of it. In an unused fragment of *Les Faux-Monnayeurs* (which Gide inserted in his *Journal*) he has Edouard say that he has discovered a new superior morality based not on allegiance to external values (religious, social, or family) but to a morality which corresponds, instead, to the needs of an inner uncontaminated being.[12]

In *Si le grain ne meurt* Gide compared himself to Prometheus:

> I was like Prometheus astonished that one could live without an eagle and without being devoured by it. After all, without knowing it, I liked that eagle (Pléiade, p. 550).

Like his fictional counterpart Gide, at least initially, compromised with his Protestant conscience (the eagle) because he had not learned how to live without it. He realized, however, that the conflict between his mother's God and his own needs might some day be resolved:

> And then it became clear to me that this harmony must be my supreme goal, and the search to acquire it the express reason of my life. When in October '93 I embarked for Algeria, it was not so much toward a new land, but toward *that*, toward that Golden Fleece, that my impulse propelled me.[13]

Les Nourritures had been too one-sidedly Nietzschean to represent the kind of "harmony" Gide later achieved in *Thésée*. It was, nevertheless, one of the phases of Gide's evolving and constantly shifting stances. Within the span of time encompassed by these two books (from 1897 to 1946) works such as *Le Retour de l'enfant prodigue*, *Les Caves du Vatican*, *La Symphonie pastorale*, *Oedipe*, and *L'Ecole des femmes* used the "dialogue" with Catholicism as a dramatic element in the narrative.

In *Les Faux-Monnayeurs* the connection is indirect though in itself interesting. Jacques Lévy, a young man of Jewish birth, was converted to Catholicism—a conversion which he attributed to the reading and the study of *Les Faux-Monnayeurs*. In his letters to his mother, written during 1934, he speaks of finding a religious faith as well as the "clue" to Gide's "non-faith." *Les Faux-Monnayeurs*, according to Lévy, is the story of Gide's conscience, the assaults made on his soul by grace, and his ultimate refusal to listen to the religious message of his own work. Lévy lists fifty-one themes, which, however, reveal more about Lévy's conversion than Gide's refusal. Lévy interprets the climax of the novel, the suicide of little Boris, as the spiritual death of Gide. The flaw in Lévy's analysis of course, is in assuming that Gide is necessarily Boris. Gide's intent was to isolate, define, describe and illustrate how the *counterfeit* in a particular social milieu could *murder* a troubled, sensitive boy. Lévy might have described more profitably André Walter's madness, Gide's symbolic murder of an earlier morality, as the beginning of a spiritual transformation.[14]

All of Gide's works are the story of his "consciences" and Boris' role is neither more nor less symbolic than Michel's, Alissa's, Oedipus', or Theseus'. The roles of each of Gide's characters, in the final analysis, balance each other and lead toward the moral harmony he sought to achieve. Nor can Gide's letter to Lévy ("I give my total assent to your point of view") be taken at face value. Many authors encourage contradictory interpretations of their work, Gide in particular. Furthermore, as Gide's biographers tell us, he was notorious for his willingness to adopt an opposing point of view even though he did not believe in it. In *Les Faux-Monnayeurs* he places the responsibility for "murder" on a counterfeit middle-class whose bourgeois Protestantism has permeated, contaminated, and directed the actions of at least three generations. Boris is the youngest member and most recent victim of this milieu. Boris' "murder" can, therefore, be interpreted as a spiritual suicide, but not Gide's. It symbolizes, rather, the destruction of certain members within the group who cannot adjust to it. Gide's anguished cry in *Si le grain ne meurt* that he is "not like the others" is a plea for the kind of understanding that a doctrinaire group generally refuses to accord the nonconformist.

The Lévy-Gide dialogue is of peripheral interest, however, since Gide made no attempt to exploit a possible opposition of values. Also, by the time Lévy began interpreting *Les Faux-Monnayeurs* Gide already had his Claudel-Jammes correspondence safely tucked away in one of his files. By 1925 there really was not much to add to a dialogue which had, for the most part, run its course. In this respect, even Gide's correspondence with Charles du Bos is singularly uninteresting. Gide refers us appropriately to Du Bos's *Journal* (Volume IV) in which anything pertinent they might have talked about in a correspondence has already been explained.

In contrast to Gide's fragmentary exchange with Lévy, his correspondence with Claudel and Jammes is of unusual interest and significance. The "dialogue" with Jammes seems to have begun in July, 1897. Jammes published an article in *Le Spectateur Catholique* entitled "En faveur de la Simplicité Chrétienne. Lettre à Ménalque sur les *Nourritures terrestres*," in which he attacked the joy and exuberance of *Les Nourritures*. In "Réponse à la lettre du Faune," published in the September 1897 issue of the same journal, Gide asked if joy must cover itself with ashes and sadness lest it offend the less fortunate. In the October issue Jammes answered Gide by saying that in the presence of the blind there must be no mention of sight, the sun, or even of the beauty of flowers. Furthermore, he advised Gide to search for Divine rather than Earthly nourishment so that one day, he too, might *pray* for his daily bread.

Jammes was not converted to Catholicism until 1905, yet Gide was already using Jammes' religious zeal as a force antagonistic to his *Nourritures*. Gide's exchange with Jammes reveals that Jammes was, in essence, asking Gide to subscribe to ideas he had already rejected in *Les Cahiers d'André Walter*. By 1897 Jammes' God is no longer Gide's. Gide's answers to Jammes' admonishments echo parts of *Les Nourritures* in which he had already proclaimed the supremacy of a Nature-God.

Gide's rebellion against dogma, the Church, and its orthodox conceptions of God, as a protestation against obedience, was comparable, in some ways, to Adam's or Prometheus' act of disobedience.

> "God is love," said St. John. No! it is not that which must be said. Say: "Love is our God," but then, which is the God who created the earth? Whether it comes from Prometheus or from Christ, the act of kindness is an act of protestation against God—which God punishes.[15]

Claude Mauriac, in his book, *Conversations avec André Gide*,[16] in dealing with the question of obedience and protestation, records an interesting exchange that took place between Gide and François Mauriac at Malagar on July 2, 1939. During one of their many discussions about the devil, Catholicism, and faith in general, Gide observed that, in the Garden of Eden, there were two trees forbidden to Adam: the tree of life and the tree of knowledge; that Adam and Eve ate only of the tree of knowledge; and that, in order to prevent man from eating from the tree of life, God chased them both from the Garden of Eden. Gide commented further that man's disobedience was the birth and beginning of consciousness and that God's commandment represented His fear of such consciousness, His sense of being threatened by it and by man, a statement with which François Mauriac concurred.

Essentially, both men were reiterating a familiar interpretation of man's fall which runs throughout much of Western literature, that is that Adam's self-consciousness, symbolically, was expressed in terms of his having eaten the fruit of the tree of knowledge until, in shame, he was forced to gird himself with fig leaves. Thus it was that to punish Adam and to prevent him from eating of the tree of life (also the source of everlasting life) God chased him from the Garden.

In view of Gide's admiration for William Blake and of Blake's assertions that the "Combats of Good & Evil is Eating of the Tree of Knowledge," and that there "is not an Error but it has a Man for its Agent," Gide's characters, who represent varying degrees of consciousness or rebellion, as well as nonconsciousness and submission, perpetuate the mythological overtones contained in Adam's initial act of disobedience. Finally, and again quoting Blake, if the "Combats of Truth & Error is Eating of the Tree of Life," [17] then Gide's rebellion against the Church, and authority in general, takes Adam's disobedience one step further. Insomuch as Gide's fictional "dialogue" describes the combats of good and evil as well as of truth and error, as he sees them, then this additional consciousness, which is a new and distinctive interpretation, means that man has eaten or is now eating of the tree of life.

But rebellion itself, for Gide, is no guarantee of everlasting life. *Les Nourritures terrestres*, in its Nietzschean exaltation of self, is a necessary prelude to a spiritual fulfillment which can only be derived, in the final analysis, through self-abnegation. If only *Les Nouvelles nourritures*

contained the lyrical mastery of the earlier *Nourritures,*
and were therefore read more frequently, Gide's admirers,
as well as his critics, would sense how important this
sequel is to the moral elaboration of Gide's thought. *Les
Nourritures terrestres* is a visceral outpouring. *Les Nouvelles nourritures* is cerebral and, therefore, one could
argue, felt less deeply. Yet, together, they represent a kind
of balance between the passions and the intellect which
Gide maintained was essential for the proper functioning
of man's total self. Artistically, the visceral is perhaps
more viable and the control of such passions less interesting whenever the intellect predominates, but the moral
balance is there and Gide, when speaking rationally, gives
them equal weight. *Les Nouvelles nourritures* incorporates
Gide's reading of Dostoevsky as well as the Gospel of St.
John.

For Gide, therefore, eating of the second tree, the tree
of life, means giving of oneself to others. The first step is
consciousness, rebellion, and self-affirmation. The second
step, once some kind of self-realization has been achieved,
is to help others in their struggle for self-realization. The
joy of total self-fulfillment then depends on having eaten
from both trees. The second, without the first, is probably
not very productive while the first, alone, is pure egoism.
The proper balance between the two satisfies man's dual
responsibility to himself as well as to others. So the "life
everlasting" which comes with eating the fruit of the
second tree is possible here and now. The joy of self-fulfillment in this double sense is the only possible eternity.

In the meantime, and at least initially, the act of diso-
beying an imperious God, who had chained man to the
Caucasus of obedience, represented the first and necessary
step toward the affirmation of man's "selfhood" which, as
far as Blake and Gide were concerned, stood for the full
force of man's individual claim to self-assertion. Gide, like
Blake, wished to destroy man's obedience to moral pre-
cepts that hindered the full power of the creative self. Like
Blake in his "Songs of Experience," Gide wished to bring
man from God the Father to God the "inner vision."

Both men show us the face of evil as a human face. But

Gide does not glorify the excesses of his characters. His purpose is to demonstrate, first, though not on as grandiose a scale as Blake's visions or the tormented quests of Dostoevsky's characters, the excesses, demonic or otherwise, of which man is capable. Second, the role of such experience is to reveal that the world is exactly what man makes of it and that man's greatest triumphs can be achieved by vision, intellect, and willful determination.

The combats that are waged within the psyches of Gide's fictional characters, their struggles with themselves, with angels, devils, passions, conscience, in short, with all the eagles devouring their livers, reveal conflicts of opposing values. Gide's works expose the faces of men tormented by such "eagles." These are works of an "experience" perhaps too harsh to be lived, but the consciousness we gain thereby makes it possible for us better to savor the "fruits of the earth." Gide hoped that eating of them might lead others toward a new Garden of Eden.

He probably did not have this total vision in mind when he first started writing *Le Traité du Narcisse*. Narcissus does dream, nevertheless, of a lost paradise. Gide's Prometheus also laments a paradise lost. Finally, in *Le Prométhée*, Angèle's gesture of going to Rome down the Boulevard, arm in arm with a naked Meliboeus, seems to point the way toward a paradise in which Gide would have his readers find happiness.

Meanwhile Gide's correspondence with Claudel and Jammes further clarifies the picture of opposing forces. According to Gide, the best way to identify the enemy was to bring him forward, either by invitation or by ruse. In a letter of July 1897 he slyly prods Jammes:

> Do you therefore love me enough to want to "save" me, dear friend? I am, you know, difficult to redeem, and thwart the designs of the Saviours! (Jammes-Gide Correspondence, p. 117).

In subsequent letters Gide either feigned readiness for conversion or commented on his work in such a way as to give Jammes "hope." We should not be too hasty, however, in accusing Gide of duplicity or insincerity. Jacques Rivière's similar coyness with Claudel actually led to his conversion. We need only compare Rivière's simultaneous correspondence with Claudel and Gide to determine Rivière's ambivalent relationship with the forces warring within him.

Toward the end of August, 1897, Jammes does manifest an interest in Gide's soul:

> Do not be at all sad at my evaluation of the *Nourritures terrestres*. It is one of the greatest genuflections before God that has been shouted forth—this book of yours, excepting a few insignificant details . . .
>
> .   .   .   .
>
> This book, understand, *you will do it again* and then you will burn these *Nourritures* because they will be in the other work—otherwise (Jammes-Gide Correspondence, p. 121).

The "insignificant details" Jammes speaks of cannot easily be minimized or, for that matter, resolved. It will soon be apparent that Gide's genuflection before his god has little resemblance to the god Jammes would have him worship. As for redoing *Les Nourritures*, we have Gide's subsequent genuflection in *Les Nouvelles nourritures*. But this version in no way negates the earlier one which is an inevitable and necessary prelude to the message contained in the sequel.

Perhaps sensing that his first letter had missed the mark, in another one, written toward the end of October 1897, Jammes changed his tone. He accused Gide of ruining *Les Nourritures*. He implored him to return to the fold, as had Verlaine: "ever since *Walter*, in spite of the enormous growth of your genius, you have gone astray" (Jammes-Gide Correspondence, p. 124).

The distance between Jammes' and Gide's values was enormous, yet Gide nurtured their friendship. Why? Why did a letter of his, written from Venice on April 17, 1898 exude irony and double-entendre? Is Gide really exploiting Jammes' naïveté?

Caro Mio,
I am moved when I think of our friendship. How beautiful it is! What a touching episode in "The History of the letters of France and all countries! . . ." If only our . . . talents were alike! . . . but no, and it is because of our divergence that our friendship is so important. Moreover, it is important in the eyes of others for what it will be worth, important in my eyes insomuch as it is inexhaustibly delicious to me. Also, your confidence in the saintly reason of your Church makes you so tenderly right! And I like to be in the position of being lectured to by you (Jammes-Gide Correspondence, p. 137).

The lightness of tone suggests a cat and mouse game through which Gide seemed to be defining the relevance of the correspondence for his future readers. Jammes, however, did not follow the lead. Commenting on a proposed trip, he wrote to Gide that he would not lecture and contradict him even though "you are happy generally when someone is annoying you" (Jammes-Gide Correspondence, p. 155). Consequently, around 1901 there was a cooling-off period in their friendship. But the publication by the Mercure de France in 1902 of Jammes' *Existences* together with *Jean de Noarrieu* as *Le Triomphe de la Vie* prompted Gide to try again. In their reviews a number of critics had alluded to Jammes' omniscience, hence Gide's reference to "the role of God."

Existences is admirable! . . .

.   .   .   .

The "role of God" is so great that one can both hate and adore him at the same time, just as one lives life itself and the innocent image of life. I am not saying that you are God, but you represent for me more than a man, and when I think of you, it is not only you I think of (Jammes-Gide Correspondence, p. 188).

It was perhaps inevitable that Gide should resume contact with a direct allusion to God. It is fairly safe to say that, when thinking of Jammes, Gide linked him with the orthodoxy he (Gide) was exposing and at the same time undermining. When Gide says that he is looking for something fresh, for a place to rest his head, he seems, once more, to be tantalizing Jammes: "I thirst for you as one thirsts for spring waters. You are the thirst-quencher; I am the fever" (Jammes-Gide Correspondence, p. 189). In this passage Gide was using a language reminiscent of *Les Nourritures*: "The greatest joys of my senses have been those of thirsts quenched" (Pléiade, p. 217). To identify Jammes, the religious zealot, with the humanistic natural-ism of *Les Nourritures* was not without irony, particularly in view of Jammes' earlier suggestion that Gide return, for sustenance, to the "nourritures divines." Gide's statement then becomes a subtle inversion, an indirect allusion, an invitation perhaps that Jammes should continue coercing him toward godliness.

Jammes' strongest efforts in this direction did not come, however, until after 1905. That was the year Jammes himself was drawn to Catholicism as a result of Claudel's influence. In the meantime his encounter with Gide prompted Jammes to write a letter to Mme. Gide. He wrote with amazement at Gide's new health in contrast to his previous debility.

> I confess to you that my mother and I were astounded to find in him such strength, the strength of a man who has rallied from an illness—we who were used to his constant liver ailments and diet of soft-boiled eggs. He took long walks without a trace of fatigue; he ate and drank in a manner that would formerly have frightened him. This was no longer the hero of the *Nourritures* who fasts in order to eat. No! He ate and drank like Cherfils when he proclaims he is a reiter. I emphasize the drink: he drank strong wines like those celebrated by Hafiz, Moréas or Gamache; he drank excellent cognac, and announced simply the next morning: I was drunk last night (Jammes-Gide Corre-spondence, p. 201).

Jammes' portrait reveals a man of inordinate vitality.

In the intervening years, from 1906 to the war of 1914, Jammes and Claudel made repeated efforts to influence Gide's religious orientation. They criticized his values more openly and they tried deliberately to weaken and disturb his sense of moral equilibrium. They even attacked his self-confidence. In a letter of April 30, 1906, for instance, Jammes compared Gide's manner and behavior to the directionless floating of a cork on water. Jammes insisted that there was only one remedy for Gide and that was a return to God.

> You are in the singular state of a man whose *"soul* has *gills"* (Claudel) necessary for the aspiration toward God and who, for years now, has absorbed through these gills a tincture of cameleon (Jammes-Gide Correspondence, p. 235).

If Gide was disturbed he showed neither impatience nor hostility, only a certain irony. In his *Journal* of May 2, 1906, he noted the following:

> Jammes has written to me on sky-blue paper a parish priest letter which reminds me of Pourceaugnac's doctors trying to persuade him that he is ill. Perhaps I am on the threshold of Paradise, but it is not at the gate he thinks it is.[18]

In fact Gide seemed quite impervious to Jammes' admonishments. In his answer of May 2, 1906, he referred to Jammes' unhappy love affair as a kind of prelude to his conversion. He wrote, not without an element of cruelty, that it must have been Jammes' broken heart which opened the doors of paradise (Jammes-Gide Correspondence, p. 236). It was already evident, even before he wrote *Le Retour de l'enfant prodigue*, that Gide viewed conversion as a definite weakness. Only the strong, only those who were self-sufficient in their inner directions, could remain outside the walls of the Church. In his *Journal* of August 8, 1905, Gide compared "the Catholic discipline" to Red Cross vehicles. "If only people tried to advance on foot instead of being carried."

In the same letter in which Gide accused Jammes of projecting an imaginary image of his (Gide's) anxiety, he referred to the useful lesson he had gleaned from reading Claudel's journal and letters, a reading which, it seems, dampened Gide's admiration for Claudel.

The reading of his journal and letters has fortunately inhibited my liking of his person and my admiration of his work. The reaction has prevailed by far over the action, and it is for *that* that I am grateful to him (Jammes-Gide Correspondence, p. 236).

The word *that* (*cela*) refers to Gide's antipathy for Claudel and his values. In a passage I quoted earlier from *Si le grain ne meurt* Gide again italicized the word *cela* thereby revealing an interesting and significant parallel. In the earlier passage the word referred to the ultimate "harmony" to be achieved by synthesizing the two extremes of Gide's personality. If Gide was "grateful" to Claudel for what he had found in his journal, it was only because this newly found antagonism would help Gide progress "artistically" toward that "harmony," toward that italicized *cela* which certain forces, by opposition, were helping to define more clearly.

In the meantime Gide had met Claudel, but a misunderstanding, probably deliberate on Gide's part, arose after a reading of one of Jammes' poems. Gide wrote to Jammes, apropos of his reaction, that he (Gide) was already entirely Catholic. Claudel and Jammes interpreted this one sentence as a "readiness" for conversion and began pressing him even harder. On August 21, 1906, Jammes wrote to Gide:

> Physically, you are robust. But God will not let go of you. He needs you too much! And his hand will bend you as it bent me, will bend you until like the Jew of Villiers, you will find only a Cross to hold on to—or, beneath your spine, the impenetrable and naked rock of Faith (Jammes-Gide Correspondence, p. 241).

In his immediate answer to Jammes, Gide implied that he was in the throes of an agonizing spiritual crisis and he wished that Jammes, with his "customary perspicacity," would reveal further intimate secrets about him (Gide) and his work. "Like the dying Sinbad straining toward the air-vent in the stifling city of the dead, I am struggling and dragging myself along" (Jammes-Gide Correspondence, p.

242). Gide's "agony," however, lacked the authentic ring of a true religious crisis. Nevertheless, Jammes answered him in October (1906) urging him not to give up:

> If you were Catholic, I would teach you how wonderful the meditation of the Rosary is, that sublime application of the merest event of everyday life to Joy, Sadness or the Glory of God (Jammes-Gide Correspondence, p. 244).

In his answer to Jammes of November 13, 1906, Gide wrote, "Do not attribute my silence to any annoyance. Your letter was good and I am your friend" (p. 245). But ten days later in his *Journal* of November 23, 1906, he wrote, "It taxes me to write to Jammes so insipidly. But what to do? . . . He has a nose only for incense." Gide was obviously toying with Jammes. It seems more and more likely, in retrospect, that his purpose was to expose the inadequacy of such proselytising and the flagrant presumption of those who would impose their faith upon others. No doubt Gide also wished to demonstrate the coexistence of opposing tendencies within himself which would, in the long run, explain the meaning of the "ultimate harmony" he was after. For the moment he was still cultivating the extremes and Jammes was the unwitting antagonist for Gide's "moral purpose": to demonstrate that the viscissitudes of self and inner turmoil were temporary states of mind and that, if man would let reason prevail, effective and lasting self-determination was possible.

Gide's allusions to organized religion, as an escape hatch from too harsh a reality, were a constant factor in his thinking. After Barrès' speech to the Académie Française in January 1907 he wrote, "Came away from there all demoralized from fatigue and sadness. Another day like that and I will be ripe for religion." [19]

In spite of Claudel's and Jammes' efforts, a return to the fold was not what Gide had in mind. In 1907 *Vers et Prose* published *Le Retour de l'enfant prodigue*, Gide's answer to Claudel and Jammes. On July 2, 1907 Gide wrote to Christian Beck to explain the genesis of his prodigal:

perhaps you don't know that Claudel, having found in Jammes a lamb easily led back to the Lord, has tried to take me in hand also. That is called "to convert," isn't it? No doubt he did not hide to himself the fact that with my heredity and Protestant education he did not have an easy task; no bother, he persevered, encouraged excessively by the very lively sympathy I showed for his work and by the resultant advantage his words had over me. We went very far, by letter and through conversation alike. Meanwhile, Jammes led me to understand that one of his articles, a dithyrambic "study" was going to celebrate my conversion. I realized that there was a risk of a misunderstanding and, resolved not to owe Jammes' praise to a moral compromise (involuntary but acknowledged), I wrote him a long explanatory letter, which led, on his part, to a brusque cooling-off. He felt that I was "escaping."

. . . .

Still, understanding to the marrow of my bones both the *interest* in the gesture that Claudel and Jammes wished me to make, and why I did not make it—and how, if I had made it, it could only have been in the manner in which *my* Prodigal Son returned to the *House*—to help the little brother leave it—I wrote that little "occasional" work in which I put all my heart, and all my reason.[20]

The Christian parable, as found in St. Luke, stresses the redemption of a sinner. The son's father and his household rejoice over the fact that the Prodigal, who has now mended his ways and has "seen the light," is ready for salvation. There is great exultation, the fatted calf is killed, and the family celebrates the young man's return to the fold.

To the original parable Gide added two characters, the mother and the younger brother. While both versions describe the joyous event of the son's return, the reasons for the return of Gide's Prodigal in no way resemble those of the Biblical version. In a series of dialogues with his father, with his older brother, with his mother, and with his younger brother, the Prodigal exposes his weakness, his laziness, his corruption, and his spinelessness. He has squandered a heritage in pursuit of pleasure: "The son confesses that he has not found happiness, nor has he been able to sustain the rapture he sought as a substitute." [21]

The Prodigal tells his mother that he was searching for his identity (in *Le Prométhée mal enchaîné* the people on the boulevard are looking for their personalities). He tells his younger brother that he was looking for freedom but admits that, at times, he did not know what he was looking for. He says, finally, that he was after the kind of thirst which only the wild pomegranate (the celebrated fruit of Gide's *Perséphone*) could provide but laments the fact that he was not strong enough to sustain this thirst. A slave to his desires and much too dependent on his father's initial allowance, now spent, he must work so hard to satisfy his needs that he decides in the end to go home. "The freedom I was seeking I lost; a captive, I had to serve" (p. 489).

In *Les Nourritures terrestres* Gide had already used the desert as an important spiritual landscape. Ultimately it was to become the symbol of harmony: a source of satisfaction as well as the means for self-abnegation (*dénuement*). The desert, by its very barrenness excludes pre-established systems and dogmas. In the Sahara the European, at least, is forced to invent new modes of survival which engender a reliance on self. The desert, symbolically, is a place in which man is constantly being challenged to reinvent himself.

Gide's Prodigal cannot adapt to the desert's austerity because, like the Saul of Gide's play, he has been eaten from within by desire. His compulsive needs, like Michel's obsessive behavior in *L'Immoraliste*, are a barrier to freedom. He realizes finally that he cannot be totally self-determined and returns, therefore, to his father's House.

In the young brother Gide has created the image of the older Prodigal but without his weaknesses. The younger brother, like the older one before him, also feels like a captive within the House. But unlike his brother he leaves with no money, no ties to corrupt him, and the now assimilated experience of his predecessor. Gide hints at the possibility that he will not duplicate the Prodigal's mistakes; that he will therefore find the necessary strength never to return. Not only does the prodigal wish his younger brother "Godspeed," but he holds the lantern high, illuminates the way, and advises him where not to stumble on the steps. These gestures and words are significant because they are the prelude to the young brother's search for himself, freedom, and happiness.

We see that the older brother returns to his Father's House so that the younger brother might be free. For the moment he still holds the lantern, because he knows where he has stumbled and failed. But he hopes that the younger brother will have the fortitude, once outside the walls, to illuminate his own way. "And you will be similar, Nathanaël, to whomever would follow the guiding light that he himself would hold in his hand" (*Les Nourritures terrestres*). Gide not only infuses this story with the symbolic desert landscape of *Les Nourritures*, he establishes a kind of parallelism between Nathanaël and the younger brother for whom he advocates a fulfillment of self based on an inner self-reliance.

Gide makes it perfectly clear in the letter to Christian Beck that he would only consider conversion for the sake of "corrupting" younger brothers within the Church. Gide's *Journal* entries and the very writing of the Prodigal story indicate not only that he refuses conversion but that, unlike the Prodigal, he has found the strength to remain outside the walls. The act of writing *Le Retour de l'enfant prodigue* represents an answer to Claudel and Jammes, an oblique attack on the Church, and a manifestation of Gide's spiritual strength and independence.

Within the specific context of Gide's dialogue with Claudel and Jammes, the House the Prodigal Son returns to is the Catholic Church. The Father is God. The older brother probably stands for the Pope, the clergy in general and, in this case, for Claudel and Jammes. Gide himself, therefore, is carrying on a dialogue with two "older brothers." But outside the specific frame of reference of Gide's correspondence the House probably symbolizes any intel-

lectual system which confines and impedes the free movement of the human mind. Aldyth Thain observes that the
older brother stands for any order or system claiming
authority over human life.[22] The figure of the mother
probably represents the eternal mother, perhaps the
Virgin Mary and, as Thain remarks, she is "the loving lap
of security where the weak find refuge."

This House (always capitalized) was not built by the
Father but by others in His name. It is the oldest brother,
like the Pope, who rules the House and who interprets the
Father for those living within its walls. "Outside of the
House," says the brother, "there is no salvation for you."
The Prodigal protests, however, that he and his brother do
not resemble each other:

> "It is your fault."
> "Why mine?"
> "Because I live within the established order; all that
> differs from it is the fruit or the seed of pride."
> "Can I differ only by faults?"
> "Call nothing quality but that which leads back to order,
> and suppress all the rest" (p. 480).

One of the reasons the Prodigal left the House was
because he feared and resented his brother's moral tyranny: "He who would understand the Father must listen
to me," says the older brother.

> "I understood Him easily without you."
> "It seemed that way; but you understood wrongly. There
> are not several ways of understanding The Father" (p.
> 481).

This exchange between the two brothers obviously represents more than personal grievance since it carries with
it one of the fundamental distinctions between Protestantism and Catholicism. Within this context the Prodigal
Son symbolizes Protestantism itself which, from Gide's
point of view, did not go far enough in emancipating itself
from Catholic dogma and the tyranny of the Pope "and I
believe, at least in this respect, that the moral ethic of the
Protestant people is more manly and vigorous than that of
the Catholics: more encouraging of effort" (*Journal*, 27

September 1942). Gide abrogated the right of the Church to be the sole arbiter of the Bible.[23]

What Gide seems to have meant, by the greater virility of Protestantism, was the act itself, the very effort of the Prodigal to explore new moral relationships outside the walls of the Church. While Gide rejected both Protestantism and Catholicism he insisted that he was profoundly Christian. In any case he retained the Protestant prerogative to interpret Christ the way he saw him.

Gide's notations in his *Journal* indicate that he always felt close to the moral teachings of Christ. Gide interpreted Christ as a rebel against institutionalized doctrine, as a man dissatisfied with the status quo, as a person who had come to teach a new road to salvation. But if Gide admired the figure of Christ he considered all "official" subsequent interpretations of his message as inadmissible distortions of what had once been a beautiful and revolutionary message. "Whether he be Saint Paul, Luther, or Calvin, I feel that God's truth is tarnished through His spokesmen." [24]

The aspects of institutionalized doctrine which Gide objected to were its dogma, stasis, and complacency: "The palace of faith . . . there you will find consolation, assurance and comfort. There everything is set up to protect your laziness and to shelter the mind from effort" (*Journal*, 7 May 1927). These are precisely the reasons Gide's Prodigal gives for his return. Living outside the walls of his Father's House was too difficult. Could he not indulge his desires, with less effort, inside the walls where the older brother will do the thinking and the interpreting of the Father for him? Big brother will then become the prophet, the person who speaks for the Father, since according to "big brother," the Father does not reveal his intentions clearly.[25]

In support of his attack on Protestantism and Catholicism Gide quotes from an article by M. Fouillée in an 1895 issue of *La Revue des Deux Mondes*:

Protestantism, after having been more reactionary even than Catholicism, decided to oppose Catholic immobility with the idea of free inquiry. As soon as they discovered that, the Protestants' cause was won—but also lost. They had sounded their opponents' deathknell; since in the face of a religion chained to itself and enveloped in the past, like a final growth wrapped in a sheath, they were establishing a free and progressive religion capable of absorbing everything that free scientific inquiry could bring to it. They held that since free inquiry had no limitations, it constituted an unlimited religion, hence indefinite and indefinable, which would not know, the day when free inquiry brought it to atheism, whether atheism was part of it or not; a religion destined to vanish in the indefinite circle of philosophism it had opened up. All liberal thought, every philosophism, all intellectual anarchy were to be found in Protestantism as soon as it stopped being a radical Catholicism.[26]

Repeatedly, Gide stated that there was a deep strain of Protestantism within him. But his insistence on the necessary and perpetual avenues of free inquiry which, in his opinion, have already substituted themselves for most forms of reactionary Protestantism, must, inevitably, continue to oppose all forms of absolutism, including radical Catholicism. Gide's dialogue with Claudel, Jammes, and company fits into the larger context of the historical evolution of Protestantism and free thought.

The ability to stand upon one's "own two feet," in contrast to the Prodigal's inability to do so, is an analogy Gide draws for the progression of mankind.

Little Edith Heurgon is beginning to walk. Never before have I witnessed anything so marvelous: The first steps of a small child. Having been held until now, all of a sudden it begins to understand that it can stand up without support, go forth alone . . . Humanity has scarcely reached this stage, still tottering, dizzied by the space yet to be covered, atilt, incompletely weaned from the milk of beliefs (*Journal*, 15 July 1943).

Gide would like to see man stand alone, unaided and unafraid. It is the rebels, he says, who will save the world, if indeed the world is going to be saved. Those who submit to the tyranny of the mind will, consciously or unconsciously, prevent man's emancipation. In a letter to Bernard Enginger, referring specifically to Catholicism and Communism, he noted:

> Worn out by yesterday's struggle, young men (and a number of their elders) look for and think that they find, in this very submission, rest, assurance, and intellectual comfort. Shy, they even seek in it a reason for living and convince themselves (or let themselves be convinced) that they will be of better service and will take on their full value, when enlisted to do so. Thus it is that, without really realizing it, or realizing it only too late, through obedience or laziness, they are going to contribute to the defeat, the ruin of the spirit.[27]

The above quotation dates from 1946, but the date itself in no way makes its meaning less relevant to the earlier period. In August 1910, at the very beginning of Gide's revealing correspondence with Claudel, he wrote, "One is willing to be on the side of the believers; but one prefers not to be on the side of the fools." [28]

On December 7, 1911 Claudel wrote to Gide asking him when he would follow Jammes' example and be converted.[29] In his answer Gide replied, "I still feel that I haven't the right to tell you of this until I make up my mind to go with you all the way" (10 December 1911, Claudel-Gide Correspondence, p. 185). This was a step Gide would never make, yet, like Prometheus fattening his eagle, he fed Claudel's hope with such tantalizing tidbits. Claudel was far more successful in converting Copeau, Cocteau, Du Bos, Ghéon, and Jacques Rivière. In fact, one of the reasons Claudel's correspondence with Rivière is so interesting is that Rivière alternately pleaded with and dared Claudel to find the right answers for him, whereas Gide seems to have used the correspondence to expose, on the one hand, Claudel's methods and, on the other, the reasons for resisting them.

Rivière is an intermediary figure within the dialogue of the giants since, as a young man, he experienced their impact and was alternately drawn toward both. He was, in fact, attracted to and repulsed by those same authoritarian-humanistic forces which had structured the Gidean dialogue from its very inception. As a result we have a dialogue within a dialogue, formed by Rivière's correspondence with both Gide and Claudel, in which he asked them to structure a reality for him.

The very nature of Gide's nonauthoritarian, relativistic view of things, considering the demands Rivière was making on such a system, when contrasted with the stability of Claudel's authoritarian faith, was bound to fail. Nevertheless, in his letters to and about Gide, Rivière emphasized their affinities: "Oh, voluptuousness, strength, love, desire, words which—like Gide—I wish to repeat forever. It is by you that I live, by you that I die. You are my life. You lift me up, you are my tendency toward God, the divine magnetism of the thing I am. Desire, desire!" [30] In a letter he wrote to Alain Fournier, Rivière described a meeting he had with Gide in 1909 during which he talked to Gide of Claudel, Nietzsche, and *Les Nourriture terrestres*:

> Never have I had the emotion of feeling that as I spoke my words the same thoughts as mine were coming alive in a person so close to me. I think that he understood me terribly, with himself.[31]

There were remarkable similarities between Rivière and Gide in spite of Rivière's strong attraction toward Claudel. In 1907 he wrote to Claudel: "For more than a year I have been living by you and in you; my bulwark, my faith, my constant preoccupation, that is you. I have adored you as much as Cébès Simon; I have prostrated myself before you, I have sought your soul with my outstretched hands." [32] Rivière speaks of a terrible anxiety, of Gide's influence, of his revolt against Catholicism, his hunger for life, his ennui, his desires, and of his discontent which he adores in spite of the suffering it engenders. He ends his letter: "Cure me, cure me, my brother, my little older brother! Be my resurrection. Here I am" (Rivière-Claudel Correspondence, p. 7). This first letter to Claudel exudes a desperate and pathetic need for guidance. In his second letter to Claudel, dated March 10, 1907, this need becomes provocative, but the basic feeling is no less persistent. "Two things will always prevent me from being Christian: The feeling of the *reality of nothingness*, and my complacency in the face of my despair" (*Ibid.*, p. 8). He even dares Claudel to destroy what he calls the "calm" of his anxiety and suffering (*Ibid.*, p. 11) yet, hidden beneath the bravado tone, one senses a desperate need for direction, certainty, and meaning (*Ibid.*, pp. 16–17). "And this departure on which Gide was unable to launch me toward other things, direct me there toward God." (*Ibid.*, p. 21).

I wonder if the ambivalent feelings expressed in Rivière's correspondence are not traceable to his fear of death, to an "inner flaw," which would perhaps explain these simultaneous longings and withdrawals. In an unpublished letter to Gide dated October 24, 1911 he says that he is full of the idea of sin, moulded by scruples and remorse, anxious about death, "too anxious," he says, "that death should not be the end of everything." [33]

Throughout his correspondence with Claudel, Rivière alternately moved toward faith and then retreated. The progression was slow, but definitive. His wife's own return to the faith probably influenced him considerably as well as the traumatic birth of their first child and the considerable dangers to her life that ensued from it. There is also the "terrifying and unexpected" visit by Claudel in the fall of 1909. As a result of these cumulative influences and events Rivière announced his return to Catholicism on Christmas Day in 1913 and publicly took communion.

In his early twenties Rivière had vacillated between a typically Gidean exaltation of self and a Claudelian devotion to mystical faith. The traditionalism of his youth brought Rivière close to the author of *Partage de Midi* and the bosom of the Church, whereas the uncharted paths of self-discovery contained in *Les Nourritures terrestres* attracted him toward unknown pleasures. As he compared these two men Rivière found that Claudel's thought seemed to swing in a circle around an immovable center while Gide's thought, with no apparent center to hold it in orbit, seemed constantly to be moving and evolving toward different foci of experience. Claudel's circle seemed comforting and secure whereas Gide's circles were disquieting. Claudel forged reality into an artistic mold to conform with his religious vision whereas Gide, though he too used the artist's prerogative of "arranging" reality, did not "force" its meaning. Rivière was initially midway between the certainty of Claudel's world, with its belief in absolute values, and Gide's relative world.

The Rivière quotations I have used will, I think reveal a resemblance between Gide's Prodigal and Rivière's return to the faith: his fear of death, his religious anxiety, his need for certainty, his own suffering and the suffering of his wife and his need for an inner calm with which to combat his spiritual masochism. While there is no reason to doubt that Rivière found serenity in the faith of his mature years, the anxieties of his youth and early manhood seem to have been resolved by it. Gide, as he defined such action in his *Prodigal*, viewed it as another example of human frailty. He considered faith as an escape valve, useful for those who could not cope with the traumas of living but unnecessary for people strong enough to live without it.

Subsequently, Rivière severely criticized the absence of suffering as one of the great *lacunae* in Gide's life and art implying, thereby, that there was a "spiritual dimension" missing in his work. But this "spiritual dimension," so necessary to Rivière's Catholicism, to his ennui, masochism, and self-torment which, by his own admission he deliberately cultivated, was so foreign to the Gidean personality that the accusation seems absurd. I see Rivière as a malcontent who would impose his own spiritual malaise on those who have outgrown it. I am not convinced, therefore, that, as Rivière says, Gide is a man without misfortune, a man "beyond conflict, beyond sharing, beyond other's hard anguish." [34]

Rivière's accusation laments the fact that Gide did not

choose the Catholic gate. This is the meaning of the "despiritualization," weightlessness, "volatilization," and absence of life through happiness for which both Rivière and Du Bos resent him.[35] While Rivière's final estimate of Gide the artist was colored by his faith, the friendship between the two men flourished and was not affected by it, probably because Rivière's faith never imposed itself upon other people with Claudel's absolute rigor. We have the paradox of a continuing friendship between Rivière and Gide and a progressive alienation between Rivière and Claudel.

In contrast to Rivière's conversion, Gide's correspondence with Claudel demonstrates how the will to self-determination can successfully resist the encroachments of as authoritarian a zealot as Claudel. In his portraits of Claudel Gide describes him as a sledge hammer; his face is without nuance, he has the neck of a bull which forms part of his head and into which passion rises to congest the brain (*Journal*, 1 December 1905). He speaks continuously and without interruption and he rejects all opinion which is not his own (*Journal*, 19 November 1912). His voice is abrupt, curt, and authoritative (*Journal*, 5 December 1905). In reaction to Claudel's literary bias Gide wrote: "Beating about him with a monstrance he devastates our literature" (*Ibid.*). Julian Green, even after his own conversion, confirmed Gide's picture of Claudel whose condescending goodness and aggressive manner often irritated his listeners. But Green excused Claudel's "benevolent" clumsiness because he approved the vigor of his faith.[36]

Claudel and Gide: it is hard to imagine two figures more different or more antipathetic. Gide: Always elusive, subtle, self-effacing, nuanced; Claudel: dogmatic, firm, direct, demanding, and self-assured. In describing Claudel Gide wrote:

> To talk with him, to try to talk with him, one is forced to interrupt him. He waits politely until you have finished your sentence, then resumes where he had left off, at the

very word, as if you had said nothing. . . . (The greatest advantage of religious faith, for the artist, is that it permits him a *boundless* pride.)

Upon leaving he gives me the address of his confessor (*Journal*, 5 December 1905).

Given the nature of their correspondence, it seems reasonably certain now that Gide was aware of the role he was playing in the "dialogue." We might even say that Gide was fortunate to have had such an illustrious opponent. Gide wrote that, if possible, one must choose "beautiful enemies." What was "beautiful" or worthy about Claudel, from Gide's point of view, was that Claudel was a great writer who also incorporated all that was antithetical to Gide. Claudel was the spokesman for dogma, authority, and the Church. Like a voice from the past, Claudel's affirmations seemed capable of irritating Gide's ascetic conscience. Exposed to Claudel's overbearing manner, Gide's psychic scars, left over from his youthful struggle for self-affirmation, seemed to ooze once again. While, during moments of spiritual "crisis," Gide seems to have suffered genuinely, in his letters he tantalizes both Claudel and Jammes with bait for conversion and then skillfully eludes them, backpedals, and loses interest.

"Exposing his liver" seems to have been a conscious, deliberately contrived affair. It produced a fascinating correspondence even though it did leave both Claudel and Jammes embittered at having been duped and outmaneuvered. In an interview with Dominique Arban published in *Combat* on March 28, 1947, Claudel makes some rather caustic remarks about Gide's alleged "sincerity."

ARBAN   "If Gide did not become converted . . ."
CLAUDEL   "It is because he would accept no guide. His
      is a dreadful example of cowardice, of weakness . . .
      Poisoners must be policed. Now, Gide is a poisoner;
      I do not say that lightly. How many letters have I
      not received from young people who have gone astray?
      At the beginning of their course towards evil, there
      is always Gide."

ARBAN   "Gide has taught all of us the value of self-integrity and lucidity with respect to the causes of our actions."

CLAUDEL   "Do you think that he truly admits the causes of his actions? Gide is fascinated by mirrors. His *Journal* is nothing but a series of poses before himself. First, when one looks at oneself, one always strikes a pose. His *Journal* is, from this point of view, a monument of insincerity."

Self-direction, that one quality Gide strove most of his life to affirm, is the *weakness* and the *cowardice* Claudel seems to accuse him of propagating. (In *Le Retour de l'enfant prodigue* Gide defined the prodigal's return to the Mother Church as an act of weakness and cowardice.) Gide's good appears to be Claudel's evil. As for the insincerity of Gide's *Journal* there is truth in Claudel's affirmation if we expect a journal to be a mirror of reality. But Gide's *Journal* is, all too frequently, a distorting mirror which, like art, exaggerates in order to communicate the reality of a particular vision. Gide's narcissism, as reflected in his *Journal*, is probably one of the more authentic reflections in it and while it does, admittedly, represent a series of poses, Claudel's reaction reads like outrage born of misunderstanding rather than intelligent criticism.

Claudel was a Catholic fundamentalist while Gide was an atheistic relativist. Claudel was concerned about Gide's soul in an afterlife while Gide was concerned with the quality of man's living soul. Claudel affirmed that God created man while Gide maintained that man's vision is capable of creating God.

> When a certain stage of history is reached, everything appears in the guise of a problem. And man's responsibility increases as that of the gods decreases.
>
> It devolves upon man alone, in the final analysis, to solve all those problems which he himself will have raised (*Journal*, 27 September 1940).

We can easily discern, behind the epistolary thrusts of these two men, who fought for the souls of Ghéon, Du Bos, and Rivière, the processes of the authoritarian and the permissive points of view. As for the conversion of their famous friends, Claudel carried the day.

In 1912 Claudel was using the same tactics with Gide as with the others. He wrote:

> like all those who are feeling their way towards conversion, you have long been under the influence of the devil, who is furious at seeing you escape from his grasp. Like all those who are nervous and sensitive in an extreme degree, you are perhaps more open than are most others to that sinister influence. This idea came to me in a lightning-flash after reading *Saül* and *The Immoralist*, and last night it came back to me (Claudel-Gide Correspondence, 29 February 1912).

Gide appears to have been fascinated as well as repelled by the presumption that every thinking person preoccupied with the questions of good and evil or of freedom and bondage must necessarily be or become a Catholic. In January of the same year (1912) he noted in his *Journal* that he would have preferred never to have known Claudel. "His friendship weighs on my thought, obligating and embarrassing it . . . I still cannot bring it upon myself to hurt him, but my thought is strengthened all the more as it offends his." [37]

Gide soon found the means, however, with which to vex Claudel. It was not merely the flip and irreverent tone with which he treated the Catholic Church and the Pope in *Les Caves du Vatican* (1914). The factor which seems to have disturbed Claudel the most was a quotation from *L'Annonce faite à Marie* which Gide had placed as an epigraph to Book III of *Les Caves*. The quotation is Violaine's answer to Pierre de Craon in the Prologue of the play. She says: "But of which King do you speak and of which Pope? For there are two and no one knows which is the real one." (This is a reference to the Great Schism of the fourteenth century, when there were two claimants to the Papacy.) The quotation appeared when the novel was first published in the *Nouvelle Revue Française* (1914) but was omitted from subsequent publications as a result of Claudel's vehement objection to it.

The allusion to a false Pope is, of course, essential to the plot of *Les Caves*. It is Julius de Baraglioul's inability to distinguish between the real Pope and the presumed false one which undermines the reality of both. Julius is convinced that the audience he had was with the false one and it is this certainty which, finally, prompts Anthime Armand Dubois' return to atheism.

> Julius gave a start.
> "My friend, you terrify me. You will surely get yourself excommunicated."
> "By whom? If it's by a false Pope, who gives a damn?"
> "And I who thought I was helping you extract some consoling virtue from this secret," Julius went on in dismay.
> "Are you kidding? . . . And who knows, maybe Fleuris-soire will find out, when he gets to heaven, that his Almighty isn't the *real one* either?" [38]

It is this element of doubt which kills Anthime's faith and sends him back to the Freemasons and the writing of his scientific articles for *La Dépêche*. Thereupon Anthime's "psychosometaphysical" limp returns and he is again partly crippled. Readers will remember that his conversion was accompanied with the casting away of his crutch. Is Gide suggesting that nonbelief deforms people and that to believe is to become whole again? Or, is he saying that nonbelief, though difficult and sometimes debilitating, accompanies man's pursuit of knowledge. The second interpretation is consistent with *Le Retour de l'enfant prodigue* as well as with Gide's other pronouncements on this issue.

In the meantime Jammes and Claudel were trying to impress upon Gide the fact that he was responsible for the "evil" emanating from his books. Jammes had objected to *Les Nourritures terrestres, Amyntas, L'Immoraliste,* and *Le Retour de l'enfant prodigue* while Claudel had referred to the devil's work in *Saül* and *L'Immoraliste*. While trying to convert him they were both attacking simultaneously the values he was stressing in this works.

Gide wanted to marry a Nietzschean vigor, spontaneity, and exaltation of self with the love, dedication, and selflessness of Christ and Dostoevsky. This would be Gide's "marriage of heaven and hell," the union of *energy*, which Blake and Dostoevsky describe as a demonic force, with *love*, so that, while the energy remains, the evil, selfish, and egoistical effect is canceled and replaced by a positive, life-affirming force.

> A constant need of reconciliation torments me; it is a failing of my mind; it is perhaps a good quality of my heart. I would like to marry Heaven and Hell, *à la* Blake; reduce antagonisms and am willing most often to see only the misunderstandings in the most ruinous and murderous oppositions.[39]

Dostoevsky's distrust of intellectuals and intelligence, his faith in "good" simple-minded folk and even idiots contrast with Nietzsche's striving for self-fulfillment at the expense of the weak, the sickly, and the inadequate. Lafcadio's "gratuitous" murder of Amédée Fleurissoire (the logical sequel to the Miglionnaire's "gratuitous" slap in *Le Prométhée mal enchaîné*) parallels Raskolnikov's murder of the old woman in order to prove his superiority and his freedom.

While the crime is comparable, the punishment is not. Lafcadio's remorse and suffering last only a day or so in contrast to Raskolnikov's long expiation. Raskolnikov's "search for God" in no way matches Lafcadio's discovery of the "Tree of Life." While it is true that Geneviève and Julius tell Lafcadio that he now has no alternative but to submit to God and the Church, Gide's editorial comment obfuscates this answer and superimposes the possibility of another solution to his guilt. "Annoying," says Gide, "that that knucklehead Julius should have been the first to inform him!" (*Les Caves*, p. 872). The last sentence of the book ends again with Gide's editorial comment: "What! is he going to renounce life? and, for the sake of

Geneviève's esteem—Geneviève, whom he esteems a little less now that she loves him a little more—for that he is still thinking of giving himself up?" (*Les Caves*, p. 873). In the previous paragraph Gide has described the fact that warmth and life will, at last, triumph over the night by announcing a dawn of new trembling realizations. It is unlikely, therefore, that, in answer to the question mark which punctuates the last sentence of the book, Lafcadio would give himself up and seek refuge in the Church. How else are we to interpret Gide's remark that Lafcadio's and Geneviève's "night of love and bliss" is the beginning of another book.

Evident as this implication might be, it is incomplete. It represents Gide's intellectual solution to the problem and leaves out his emotional involvement. On the intellectual level *Les Caves* represents the reasoned solution of self-fulfillment and self-abnegation so clearly indicated in Gide's book on Dostoevsky, while on the emotional level Gide confronts us with the impasse of his sexual dilemma.

Gide intervenes frequently in the narrative of *Les Caves* to comment on the actions of the characters. His spoof of Anthime Armand Dubois, as well as of Amédée and Julius, reveals how critical he is of them, yet nowhere in the book does he intervene as flagrantly as he does at the end where he writes: "O palpable truth of desire! in the half-light you drive off the phantoms of my mind" (*Les Caves*, p. 873). The possessive adjective "my" belongs to none of the characters and, coming as it does, after Gide's "Here begins a new book," can only be an expression of the phantoms of Gide's mind. We know that most of the time Gide uses the word "desire" when other people mean love. Desire, therefore, is pushing back the phantoms of his mind. What is this "desire?" Gide tells us that "desire" is looking at the trembling tree in the garden and not at Geneviève's perfect, beautiful, and naked body. It is obvious that a Lafcadio-Gide prefers the new vistas of the symbolic tree to an already consummated love with Geneviève. As for the phantoms, Geneviève says, "the Church is there to prescribe your penance and to help you find peace through repentance" (*Les Caves*, p. 872). Since Gide has injected "his desire" so blatantly into the ending of the story, his "disponsibilité," as well as his revulsion to the Church, explain why Lafcadio's remorse only lasts a few hours and why his love for Geneviève is already on the wane. We are reminded of the solution offered by the *Tentative amoureuse* in which love (desire?), once possessed, is to be discarded for new and future encounters.

Lafcadio moves onward and away from what Gide envisages as the "prison of the Church" since it can offer nothing but phantoms. The ending of *Les Caves* expresses, once again, in classical form, the duality between emotion and intellect, between the body and the mind, the two poles of Gide's self and his art which he was still trying to resolve and which he obviously had not. The intellectual solution is there, yet, as in *Saül*, the emotional leitmotif of his sexuality breaks through.

Gide's dialogue with his Catholic opponents was therefore constantly plagued with misunderstandings. While Gide was defending the reasoned intellectual solution his works offered on one level, his opponents were attacking the undercurrent of anarchy and sexuality to be found on other levels. So when Gide criticizes social hypocrisy in his letters to Claudel, he does have the editorial comment of his books to support him.

> But how could she [Geneviève] tell him [Lafcadio] that she too, until this very day, was struggling as if in a dream—a dream from which she escaped occasionally only at the Hospital, where, tending to the real wounds of those poor children, she seemed at times to establish contact at last with some measure of reality—a mediocre dream in which her parents stirred and moved about her, all the absurd conventions of their world confronted her, and in which she could never manage to take seriously their gestures, nor their opinions, ambitions, principles, not even their very person. So why should it be surprising that Lafcadio had not taken Fleurissoire seriously! (*Les Caves*, pp. 872–73).

It is Lafcadio's refusal to take certain people seriously which explains the tone of the book and the handling, bordering on farce, of most of the characters. It is a modified Nietzschean dimension of the superman as well as a certain demonic will to experiment, which lead Lafcadio to murder. Paradoxically, it is this one act which will lift him out of his "dream world" into reality. His so-called gratuitous act, his "unmotivated murder," brings him back to himself and links him inextricably with the victim. Except for Protos and Carola (the swindler and the prostitute) all of the characters in *Les Caves* are members, by blood or marriage, of one family. Within this capsule image of society Gide would demonstrate the broader concept of society as a closely knit organism within which individual acts have unexpected and unpremeditated repercussions.

A circuitous determinism relates Lafcadio's murder to Protos and to his half-brother Julius, who is Amédée's brother-in-law. Carola, Lafcadio's former mistress, loves Amédée and denounces Protos whom Lafcadio once knew in school. The circle is now complete, and by demonstrating how the behavior of one person affects the behavior of others, or how one act generates repercussive actions, like shock waves or ripples on the surface of water, Gide proves the impossibility of a gratuitous act ever being realized.

While Lafcadio's murder lifts him into reality, Geneviève's opposing actions, her ministering to the poor and the needy, lifts her out of the quagmire of social duplicity into the same reality where the two meet. Earlier, it is Lafcadio who saves the children from the fire and Geneviève who rewards him with her purse which Lafcadio then magnanimously gives to the despairing mother. None of the other spectators at the scene of the burning building seem even remotely capable of rising to the occasion.

The intellectual level of the book, then, reads as follows: Lafcadio's repentance, guilt, and suffering, though of short duration, are sincere and are redeemed and expiated by Geneviève. Lafcadio's and Geneviève's love, the symbolic union of two opposing life forces (not to mention the comic, though perhaps equally symbolic union of Amédée and Carola), is a blend of spontaneity and self-lessness which lead now to the "life everlasting."

Gide's book on Dostoevsky is a further clarification of this "marriage" of ideas, since the Dostoevsky book, for Gide, is "a pretext to express my own thoughts." [40] While eluci-dating Dostoevsky, his correspondence, and his books, Gide is commenting obliquely on vital directions in his own works. What fascinates him in certain Dostoevsky characters is the coexistence of the same contradictory attitudes he (Gide) himself cultivates. According to Gide, Dostoevsky stresses self-abnegation—the same abnegation which is such an important part of *Les Nouvelles nourri-tures*—while Nietzsche stresses the self-affirmation which gives *Les Nourritures terrestres* its particular flavor (*Dos-toïevsky*, pp. 207–8). Raskolnikov's superman exercises his superiority at the expense of others, but Kirilov's act of suicide does so at his expense. The humanity he is going to vanquish is his own.

Geneviève's devotion to the poor and the sick makes her a kindred Dostoevsky soul, but she differs from him in that Gide makes her also a spokesman for the Church. Why? Is it Gide's restlessness, his need to move on to something new and different, or his homosexuality which prompts him to give this final conventional imprint to a character who is in every other way unconventional? Or is *Les Caves* an additional answer to and rejection of the likes of Claudel? Probably both. Obviously a more clearly defined and less ambiguous union between Lafcadio and Geneviève would better fit the Dostoevsky book and the *Nouvelles nourritures*.

Just as Lafcadio was vexed by Geneviève's Catholicism Gide was no doubt thrilled to discover in Dostoevsky an anti-Catholicism similar to his own (*Dostoïevsky*, p. 180).

"the Western World has lost Christ," writes Gide quoting Dostoevsky, "and because of this, only because of this, the Western World is crumbling." What French Catholic would not applaud . . . were he not brought up sharply against the phrase which I omitted at the beginning: "Christ has been lost,—*by the error of Catholicism*" (*Dostoïevsky*, p. 39).

One can readily imagine Claudel objecting to a statement such as this. He also objected to Gide's sexual idiosyncracies. This is why, in his letter to Claudel of March 7, 1914 Gide asks Claudel not to interpret his allusion to social hypocrisy as any kind of reference to homosexuality. Yet in his answer of March 9 this is precisely the point on which Claudel attacks him:

> No, you know quite well that the habits of which you tell me are neither permitted, nor excusable, nor avowable. You will have against you both *Revelation* and the natural order of things.
>
> . . . .
>
> I deny that the individual has the right to be both judge and defendant in his own case. The devil, pride, and the passion that holds us in its claws—all these are quick to whisper pretexts and excuses in our ear . . .
>
> . . . .
>
> . . . The vice of which you speak is spreading wider and wider. . . . you will have accounts to settle, both in this world and in the next.
>
> For your own personal interest:
>
> I tell you again: *you will be lost.* You will lose all position, you will become an outcast among other outcasts, rejected by humanity.

It is difficult to imagine that Gide would take the tone of such letters seriously. They have all the markings of dogmatic stereotype: exhortations in the name of Revelation and natural reason, the denial of the right of self determination and, finally, the categorical condemnation in the name of humanity. This is the language one addresses perhaps to wayward school boys, and Claudel generally knew better than to let such passion dominate his reason. His letters to Rivière, in contrast to many letters to Gide, reveal the workings of an intelligent mind plotting the kind of strategy which will achieve optimal results.

In the meantime Claudel wrote to Rivière, on March

27, 1914, suggesting that Gide see a competent nerve specialist, Doctor Bucher of Strasbourg, because Claudel felt that Gide was on the verge of a complete breakdown and total despair (Claudel-Gide Correspondence, p. 232). However, the moment he saw *Les Caves du Vatican* he changed his mind. He wrote to Rivière apropos of the epigraph from *l'Annonce faite à Marie:* "it has been very unpleasant for me to appear on the same cover as that disgrace" (Hambourg, 20 April 1914, Claudel-Gide Correspondence, p. 233).

Jammes, along with Claudel, also admonished Gide:

> You wanted to sing the praises of joy, and yet your works, since the *Nourritures* have been but one long, sickly, rending shudder for you . . .
>
> .   .   .   .
>
> . . . You know that leprosy can be cured. Humble yourself, for that. Abdicate yourself in order to be someone. Repent.[41]

Three days later Jammes wrote again:

> I have meditated a great deal, but simply, on your case:
>   Either you will go mad.
>   Or you will be converted; and if you do go mad, it will be, I am afraid, very much your own fault.[42]

For the moment, at least, Gide remained undisturbed by the virulence of the attacks though others, it seems, were more affected by them than he was. One evening, Claudel, in the presence of his godchild Paul Jammes, lit a "crêpe," and, while it was flaming, announced that God would similarly dispatch Gide. Paul Jammes who, at the time, did not know Gide, was so impressed by the scene that when eventually he had occasion to write Gide he said, "Surely, such people [Catholics] are frightful, and I can love only those of your ilk." [43]

Gide maintained that for friends we should let others choose us, but that *we* should choose our enemies. As early as June 1909, and perhaps anticipating the outcome of Claudel's attempts to convert him, Gide wrote to Francis Jammes saying that "the beauty of a victory is measured by the importance of the enemy vanquished" (Jammes-Gide Correspondence, p. 260). While Gide does in fact appear to have chosen Claudel and Jammes as antagonists, it was Charles Du Bos, on the other hand who, after his conversion, chose Gide. In spite of his previous friendship with Gide, and now miffed by Claudel's and Jammes' failure to influence the great corrupter, Du Bos picked up where the other two left off.

> It is surprising (but true, that Gide was favored to such an extent by the absence of class of his adversaries that there is not one of these attacks directed against him which he did not bend to his own advantage), that there was no one to tell him quite calmly: "The Counterfeiter is you." [44]

Du Bos's statement, not without vainglory, suggests that he was bound to succeed where others had failed. Gide had been saying that the values one adopts must be self-generated and that to accept a social ethic which was in conflict with one's own was one of the manifestations of the counterfeit. Du Bos's Catholicism maintained the opposite. So it was natural that he, like Massis, should accuse Gide of reversing the values of a long-established moral and social tradition:

> between good and evil he has reversed the terms, treating evil as good and good as evil, and *seeing in the good particularly* the major temptation to which it is supremely important not to give in (Du Bos, *Journal*, p. 147).

Gide's opponents, while labeling him demonic and perverse, made a big issue of his conversion as a desirable end in itself, but there is little enlightened comment on the meaning of the self-directed versus the outer-directed personality—the central issue in Gide's thought. Instead, much was made of Gide's lack of faith in a transcendent being, as though his opponents expected the very weight of transcendence to tip the scales in their favor. Renouvier's epigraph to Benda's *La Trahison des clercs*, "the

world is suffering from the absence of faith in a transcendent truth," was a veritable battle cry for those attacking
Gide and the deification of man.

The moment Gide's role was defined as demonic it was
relatively easy to proceed with the denunciation of his
works. It was such an easy formula: Gide is Satan. Satan is
evil, therefore Gide is evil. Du Bos, as literary critic, errs
even further by identifying Gide with the demonic quali-
ties of his fictional characters. He regrets, for instance,
that Gide abandoned the abstract religious tone of *Les
Cahiers d'André Walter* in order to focus on *Les Nourritures terrestres* and the kind of writing which would allow
him to develop in the direction of every conceivable excess
"where . . . the mind of the devil finds so many stepping
stones" (*Journal*, p. 82).

Whether shortsightedly, or deliberately, because of the
polemic involved, Du Bos fails to mention that Gide does
not subscribe to the excesses of his characters. Nor must we
forget that Gide's refusal to condone these excesses was
one of the central themes of his work. If moral excess is
indeed one of the foci of Gide's art, is not Du Bos
falsifying the picture by pretending that Gide subscribes
to the follies of these fictional creations? Their passions,
their fears, their desires—their very blindness are the eagles Gide would have us kill. Gide advises us to nourish
such eagles in our imaginations, if we are artists, so that in
the end we may serve them slaughtered and dressed for
the artistic repast.

Gide, however, refused the mad "experiments" toward
which he pushed so many of his characters. It is one of the
weaknesses of the attacks leveled against him that his
opponents failed to make such an important distinction.
Not only is the Catholic attack on Gide critically and
logically unsound, it never really defined the psychological
basis of his anti-authoritarianism and, as a corollary, his
passionate striving for freedom. For instance, one of the
dominant themes at the end of *Si le grain ne meurt* (after
his mother's death) is Gide's sudden feeling of liberation.
It literally bursts forth as he describes giving away his

mother's belongings (even her most cherished jewelry), to the most distant relatives. Instead of grief, and in spite of a temporary loss of orientation, he finds in her death a sense of overwhelming joy. "This freedom . . . dizzied me like the wind from the main" (p. 612).

Du Bos describes Gide's liberation as a sin against the Spirit, an emancipation which, for Du Bos, is only one step removed from cohabitation with the devil.

> Gide himself recognizes the fact that the evil Prince is methodically establishing Hell within him. This will lead me to Maritain's expression in *Grandeur et Misère de la métaphysique:* "The devil also has his martyrs," and I shall affirm that this is the zone of both Gide's tragedy and martyrdom (*Journal*, p. 190).

While referring to the *Journal des Faux-Monnayeurs* Du Bos might also have quoted the passage (p. 81, Paris, Gallimard, 1927) in which Gide says that what is missing from each one of his heroes is that tiny bit of common sense which prevents him, Gide, from following in their footsteps.

The last five pages of the *Journal des Faux-Monnayeurs* would indeed seem to suggest, at first glance, as Du Bos affirms, that Gide is admitting the devil's pernicious influence: "Certain days I feel within me such an invasion of evil that it already seems to me the evil prince is methodically establishing Hell there." [45] But can we forget the special creative energizing force with which Gide, like Blake, imbues certain kinds of evil? As an example of Gide the devil, his critics frequently refer to the "train episode" of his honeymoon. At successive stops Gide, as he himself tells the story, "flirted" with three young boys in the compartment next to the one occupied by himself and Madeleine. Later, after the newlyweds reached their destination Madeleine told him that during his "flirtation," he looked either mad or like a criminal. Gide's editorial comment stresses the fact that he was not thinking nor acting responsibly: "There was a devil in me." [46]

This episode is exhibit A for the prosecution. Their

general tone is "Shame! Abandon God, follow Satan, and you too will behave like Gide." It is not likely, however, that in his *Journal* Gide gives himself a dimension which deliberately relates him to the characters in his fiction. Since there are few, if any, gratuitous elements in Gide's work, I would suggest that he has narrated this incident for the edification of his readers. Is Gide not saying, in contrast to what his critics have generally affirmed, that we should *not* allow ourselves to be possessed by devils, passions, or eagles? Is he not saying that had he been able to reason that day in the train, he would not have behaved in such a manner? King Saul (in Gide's play) need not have failed had he, like Gide, been able to exorcise his demons. So while Gide the man admits periodic lapses of lust and passion he is by no means their slave. His fiction, including the eloquent *Retour de l'enfant prodigue*, teaches us to accept our desires but also to avoid being victimized by them.

Admittedly Gide's homosexual experiences are the liveliest narrative episodes of *Si le grain ne meurt*. Gide did not, however, as Du Bos affirms, write his "confessional" for the pleasure of exposing these "unsavory" passages. Gide's childhood, the tyrannical role of his mother, her death, his sense of liberation from her dominion lead toward and explain the exaltation of the final passages of the book.

Gide's *Journal* entries deplore the fact that, in literature, the reactionary Catholic critic should assume a tone of assurance which no critic outside the Soviet Union would dare use. He notes, not without irony, that faith, in order to manifest its zeal, makes pronouncements which are not mere judgments, but verdicts literally hurled from heaven. By 1930 Gide had concluded that his Catholic opponents would always condemn his books in the name of higher authority (*Journal*, 29 July 1930).

All this persuades me even further that when you fight in the name of religion, the certitude you have (which you must have) that the adversary is in error, and that the error is and can only be his, justifies the use of any weapon, any parry, any blow.[47]

Henri Massis' attacks on Gide in 1921 and 1924 constitute more than two thirds of his book *D'André Gide à Marcel Proust* (Paris, Lardanchet, 1958). Massis, a neo-thomist, insisted, like Du Bos, that Gide's substitution of evil for good was part of a demoniacal reversal of values. Massis also concurred with Gabriel Marcel that "Gide's immorality"

> was one of the worst sophisms in whose name the spirit of corruption has been exercised on so many helpless souls and, in its offensive, depends upon indisputably noble scruples only to turn them against themselves and make them work for the profit of powers bent on our destruction.[48]

Gide, whom Massis identified as a destroyer of classical cultural values, was also denounced, in the name of Corneille and Racine, for his "morbid sensitivity" (p. 107).

While Massis apologizes for having written 280 pages on a man whose very name should be anathema, he justifies his enterprise by saying that Gide has challenged the values on which our civilization has been built: "It is the drama of our civilization which is being acted out, as in a microcosm, within the person of André Gide" (Massis, p. 234). This is an interesting admission. On the one hand Massis writes of the "defeat of Andre Gide" while on the other he reluctantly admits his importance. Yet both he and Claudel did their best to minimize it. Claudel's catch phrase "evil is not creative" (along with "Gide's satanism," and "Gide's immorality") was part of the campaign. "Man, in order *to be* morally and to unfold according to his nature, must remain within the order of what is good" (Massis, p. 125). Such a statement assumes that the good has been pre-established and preordained; that there is one human nature and that Massis and Claudel know what it is. "Evil," writes Massis, "or human misfortune is indeed nothing else, than the 'absence' of one or more conditions which constitute the good" (p. 124). But these are circular arguments comparable to the thought of Azaïs in *Les Faux-Monnayeurs* who would dismiss the very existence of evil. Claudel's assertion that *evil* is not creative cannot be taken seriously. *Evil* is just as resourceful as the good, perhaps more so.

The a priori nature of Massis' moral system was clearly revealed during the famous debate which took place soon after Gide's "conversion" to communism and which was organized by l'Union pour la Vérité, 26 January 1935, rue Visconti, Paris, as "Un Entretien sur André Gide et son Temps." Massis (the others present were Gabriel Marcel, Jacques Maritain, François Mauriac, Jean Guéhenno, René Gillouin, Daniel Halévy, Thierry Maulnier) asserted that "the notion of man is not to be doubted, since it is a question basically of knowing the first principles which are founded on the very premises of common sense" (Massis, pp. 244–45). Ramon Fernandez opposed Massis on this definition of man, but Massis insisted that there was "a natural metaphysics of the human mind (spirit)" (p. 245). Gide answered: "This is indeed extremely serious. What has struck me constantly, was the fact that there are in man forces considered as evil which, nevertheless, can become, in turn, forceful and progressive elements." Fernandez: "That is the question; there is no avoiding it." Massis: "*If there is no avoiding it . . . it is because we cannot escape from God,* and by God I mean our personal God and not Spinoza's God. Impossible to elude this mystery which is at the center of our Being and on which all morality is founded" (Massis, pp. 245–46).

The debate between Gide and Massis or between Gide and the Catholics seems to end here, exactly where it began, in spite of subsequent flurries with Mauriac, Massis, and others.[49] Gide, the relativist, does not believe in absolutes. Massis believes in absolutes and in the knowledge of "first principles." According to him values cannot be relative since they have their source in God.

If an argument is always to return to its point of departure, if it is inevitably to end in an impasse of contradictory values, then there is probably not much point in the dialogue. This was perhaps Gide's conclusion also since, after 1935, his *Journal* entries reveal a hardening of his attitude toward Catholicism.

In this extended dialogue Gide, almost without exception, preferred to generalize the antagonisms in order to stress the universality of the conflict. Such a procedure was, I feel, deliberate and he intentionally drew attention to an issue which went beyond the purely personal in order to emphasize the broad and durable aspects of such a confrontation. Massis is, therefore, simply wrong when he asserts that Gide fails to abstract the "dialogue." On the contrary, the Gidean dialogue was forever polarizing itself in terms of the humanistic-authoritarian dichotomy.

During the course of his long "Catholic dialogue" Gide had spoken of his friends' conversion as an affliction comparable to being gassed at the front. If we look at the metaphors and analogies which Gide uses for the relationship between Catholicism and the people he has known, he describes it as a flaw, a defect, a weakness, cowardice, a contamination, a disease and, finally, apropos of Madeleine, he compares its influence to the slow progression of gangrene.[50] From Gide's bias, if Catholicism is a faith capable of giving strength, it does so only to confirm the missionary zeal of proselytizers like Claudel.

> It is curious that Catholicism, for the three converted artists I have known the best, Ghéon, Claudel and Jammes, has done nothing but encourage their pride. Communion infatuates them (*Journal*, 10 September 1922).

The conversion of his other friends Gide interprets as a search for security. They, like the prodigal, find refuge in the bosom of the Church. If Gide refuses conversion it is due, perhaps entirely, to his strong allegiance to the principles of a humanistic ethic: "I have always thought that it is to ourselves, particularly, that we must remain true" (*Journal*, 26 December 1921).

By far the most succinct and revealing commentary on the whole problem of Gide's conversion is to be found in his own *Journal* where he addresses himself to "several new converts":

> I have finally understood why I cannot and will not be one of you. My heart was on your side, and the sympathy I had for you was one of the great weaknesses of my life. I feared, I curbed every incursion of my thoughts which threatened to hurt you; I dared no longer even breathe. We have talked interminably; you know my probity; I am grateful to you for not having doubted it. We have argued; I am not skillful in defending myself; besides, you hardly even attacked me: you tried simply to get me to think as you did, ever since you began to think like the rest of them, to think without being free. You asked me to accept what you yourselves had accepted, something which seemed like a lie to me but which seemed to you like the Truth. I quickly came to the realization that we could never agree. You accused my resistance of being pride and you felt justified in condemning it. You were angered when I said: "I will let you have the last word," since it seemed to you then, as they say in fencing: I was disengaging. Well! yes; I wish to disengage. What is the use of reasoning with someone who argues: the proof that I am right is that it is written: ". . ." . . . [sic] I too have been brought up on the Scriptures; if they have informed me differently, you said it was because I was interpreting them. The proof that I was wrong was that you could not err since your thoughts were those of the Church.[51]

Gide is overly modest when he says that he defends himself badly, nor is his "dialogue" as innocent at self-defense or devoid of literary intent as he would have us believe. Otherwise, it seems to me, Gide's analysis of the "Catholic dialogue" is correct. I would add that in the face of Du Bos's and Rivière's accusations of "despiritualization" Gide elaborates *Les Nourritures terrestres* in harmony with *Les Nouvelles nourritures* and Nietzsche in harmony with Dostoevsky. The harmony he envisaged and toward which he strove, this frequently italicized *cela* he alludes to as one of the goals of his life, is the Golden Fleece—the moral balance he would maintain between reason and the passions.

The most beautiful things are those that madness prompts and that reason writes. You must remain between the two, close to madness when you dream and close to reason when you write.[52]

The premises of this balance do not coincide with the values of his Catholic critics. From the framework of humanistic ethics, however, Gide's moral position is sound and the Vatican condemnation that appeared in *l'Osservatore Romano* extreme. Metaphorically speaking Claudel, Jammes, Du Bos, Rivière, and Massis are so many eagles whose nest is the mother Church and from whose heights, each one in turn attempts either to convert Gide or to deflect his message. The purpose of Gide's dialogue with the "enemy" is at least twofold: first, to demonstrate that he, like Prometheus, is absolutely free, and second, once this freedom has been demonstrated, to engage the "enemy" on his own ground with a vocabulary and dialectic of the "enemy's" own making. What was divine becomes human. What was autocratic becomes permissive. What was Evil becomes Good. This phase of Gide's "dialogue" was certainly written with feathers from Catholic eagles.

7

Counterfeiters

In spite of Gide's "Catholic dialogue," which is a social phenomenon, some critics have lamented the absence of social dimension in Gide's fiction. Gide himself was aware of such a lacuna since he frequently admired the great tradition of the English novel and repeatedly praised the works of Fielding, Hardy, Thackeray, Dickens, and Defoe. *Les Caves du Vatican* was Gide's attempt to move beyond the purely moral dialogue of his characters into the more difficult (for Gide) artistic complexities of social intercourse. I have discussed *Les Caves* primarily as a phenomenon of Gide's "Catholic dialogue" but it obviously is much more than that insomuch as Gide, for the first time, was trying to stress (in spite of the farce) the intricate determinism of group dynamics. The gratuity of Lafcadio's murder is annihilated by the unforeseen social repercussions of an act which was to have remained supremely uncomplicated, free, and uninvolved.

While Gide still favors the role of the bastard in society, since Lafcadio becomes Bernard in *Les Faux-Monnayeurs*, Lafcadio's playfulness is muted by the array and variety of social pressures Gide brings to bear on the development of his only "novel." The counterfeit theme of *Les Caves*, presented as Anthime Armand Dubois's inability to distinguish the real Pope from the false one, is amplified in *Les Faux-Monnayeurs* to include all of the social forces which inadvertently conspire to thwart the natural growth of the individual. The theme of moral authoritarianism has now transformed itself into social determinism whose inhibiting effect on the development of the child is as baneful an influence as dogma. Society is therefore to blame for Boris' "suicide." In Gide's terms, the responsibility or lack of responsibility of society to the individual, in some cases, transforms suicide into murder.

What, according to Gide, are these counterfeit elements in society which, like the interiorized eagles we have already analyzed, can warp or destroy the individual? Gide compares social pressures to the effect of a forest on a new tree. It's most effective recourse for survival is to escape upwards toward the light. Otherwise the tree will remain warped, stunted, or deformed. *Les Faux-Monnayeurs* in Gide's exposé of the intricate mechanisms of social duplicity which warp and stunt people.

While all the characters in this novel, since there are so many, could not possibly be related as they were in *Les Caves* (except for Protos and Carola), they are nevertheless from the same upper bourgeois milieu. Many of the characters have curious and intricate relationships traceable to the Vedel-Azaïs clan which is the most flagrant example of family hypocrisy and from which the strongest counterfeit element seems to emanate.

Gide's interest in authentic beings led him, throughout his early literary career, to create characters whose dialogue was primarily with themselves or with God. André Walter converses with his soul, Alissa talks primarily with God, Michel (while influenced by Ménalque) has a running tête-à-tête mostly with himself. Though the persona of *Les Nourritures terrestres* addresses itself to Nathanaël and through him to youth in general, the discoveries this inner voice preaches are those of a long, involuted dialogue with the self which has at last discovered that the world can be beautiful. *Paludes, Le Voyage d'Urien, El Hadj, Amyntas, Saül* all represent varying journeys of the self in its search for meaning and identity.

The obstacles to self-fulfillment that the characters encounter in this early fiction of Gide's are primarily moral and psychological. The fatal flaw is within them. It is a contamination of the self which spreads like a disease growing in a climate of religious and moral absolutism.

Le Retour de l'enfant prodigue and *La Symphonie pas-*

torale allude to difficulties in the home and present the obstacles to "sincerity" as, at least in part, generated by misunderstandings within the family. But the central problem remains religious.

Not until *Les Faux-Monnayeurs* will Gide attempt to master the fictional multiplicities of a complex social reality. The novel is brought into focus by Edouard, thirty-six, a novelist who, like Gide, is also writing a novel called *Les Faux-Monnayeurs*.

Edouard's age relates him ideally to the younger eighteen-year-old generation of Bernard, Vincent, and Armand while, at the same time, making it possible for him to communicate with their parents, Profitendieu (meaning he who draws profit from God), Molinier, and Vedel. Boris' grandfather, La Pérouse, was Edouard's former teacher while Vincent, who impregnates Laura, is Edouard's nephew. Edouard is also the uncle of Strouvilhou (rhymes with *filou*, swindler), the actual coiner. Edouard used to love Laura while Vincent, whom she loves, abandons her for Lady Lilian Griffith (an extension of Lilith, the she-devil of Talmudic lore but also *griffe*, meaning claw). Lady Griffith destroys Vincent, morally and spiritually, but he takes his revenge, since he now thinks he is the devil, by drowning her somewhere in darkest Africa. The theme of responsibility is clearly indicated with the graphic story of the lifeboat in which the survivors chop off the fingers of those drowning who would capsize the boat and endanger all if they were to climb into it.

Vincent chooses to save himself and abandon Laura. His passion for Lady Griffith (his eagle) ruins him while she symbolically drowns in a boat "accident" on an African river. Egoistical self-fulfillment triumphs momentarily but is not allowed to survive without its necessary Christian corollary of responsibility to others. Vincent must, in his madness, believe he is the devil since he has been cultivating this dimension in himself to the exclusion of a meaningful counterpart—the self-abnegation stressed in *Les Nouvelles nourritures*.

Edouard represents a midpoint between two separate generations of adolescents and parents. He has lived in the Pension Azaïs where Strouvilhou has spent some time and where little Boris finally goes before he is victimized by the gang. The emphasis on different generations is important because of the parents' duplicity. The Profitendieu and Molinier families silence a potentially scandalous affair by closing the brothels which have been attracting their teenage boys. The adulterous Molinier father, abetted by his wife, is intent on saving face. The imbroglios of the Passavant and La Pérouse families reveal a pattern of hypocrisy and disunity beneath a show of honorability.

The most flagrant case of counterfeit morality is to be found in the Pension Azaïs where old Azaïs' authoritarianism holds sway. He is a naïve and puritanical patriarch whose hypocrisy is a form of blindness. He interprets the vicious activities of the gang of schoolboys as a pure effort toward goodness. Evil for him either does not exist or, if it does, he must pretend that it does not. The boys at the Pension must practice the "power of positive thinking" because Azaïs wills it and because he believes that man's daily routine can be structured into a perfect mold of social, moral, and intellectual harmony. Azaïs will not admit that his personal myth is not reality itself. His is an involuntary duplicity which may be the most difficult to resist because it believes itself sincere.

In his *Journal des Faux-Monnayeurs* Gide says that the greatest "hypocrite" is the man who lies with sincerity because he is not aware of his deception. Thus we have a diminishing scale of duplicity ranging from Azaïs to the Pastor Vedel who closes his eyes to the doubts that besiege him in order not to disturb the mechanical function of his daily routine, to the parents who proclaim the myth of family unity, sexual morality, and childhood innocence, to the psychoanalyst Sophroniska who believes that to expose evil is already to be rid of it, to Lady Griffith who does not care about the evil or harm she inflicts upon others as long as her needs are satisfied, to Strouvilhou, the actual counterfeiter and social outcast who, in his

lucid pact with evil, apes the pretense of society by distrib-
uting false currency. Gide's irony is that Strouvilhou's
"currency" is more sincere than the sham of social insincerity practiced by the parents or older people he is writing about. Most of the characters, like Edouard, are "bad
novelists" because they either reject reality, or falsify it, or
don't know what to do with it.

The older generation is therefore to blame for the distortion of reality that slowly becomes operative in the
children. The *big lie* reigns supreme. The truth, that is
reality, is falsified either inadvertently or on purpose and
the children are soon contaminated. Bernard must force
drawers (like Theseus lifting rocks) and steal suitcases in
order to discover the facts about himself and about Laura.
The truth is not easily revealed and his acts are symbolic
of how jealously the adult world guards its secrets and
perpetuates the counterfeit.

By obliquely comparing the alleged true currency with
the false Gide is, in essence, asking the reader to evaluate
both. The conclusion is not so much that the actual
counterfeit currency is false, since it imitates what passes
for valid currency, but that the money in circulation is not
worth very much either. The title of the novel symbolizes
a reality which impinges on the lives of everybody and
which Edouard does not recognize. Since Edouard does
not use Boris' "suicide" in the novel he is writing he fails
to interpret its meaning.

Boris' problem, like society's problem, is hidden. It
must be probed, delved, and brought to the surface. One
of the specific issues Gide seems to be after is a certain
inherent but repressed sexuality. Sophroniska talks to
Boris about his masturbation expecting that, once exposed, it will remedy itself, whereas, on the contrary, the
cause of Boris' "secret activities" is repressed even further.
Her psychoanalytic sleuthing is comparable to Profitendieu's who thinks that by closing the houses of prostitu-
tion where the boys have been having their orgies, the
symptom of whatever is wrong will go away. So, in effect,
Sophroniska's therapy, like society, represses Boris' sex

urge. Gide seems to be saying that sex, even in its precocious manifestations, exists, and therefore must be recognized and coped with rather than repressed, hidden or
dismissed, because the moment it is, it goes underground
where, from pure energy, it transforms itself into evil.
With no more "innocent" orgies to absorb their sexuality
the students become the accomplices of the counterfeiters.
Profitendieu stops that activity also and manages to
frighten the boys thoroughly. Repressed once more, the
energies of Georges Molinier, Ghéridanisol and the gang
of fourteen- to sixteen-year-olds turns to sadism. They
attack Boris.

In the meantime Sophroniska has inadvertently prepared Boris to be their victim. She talks about Boris' guilt
without resolving it. The guilt is therefore brought to the
surface but because nothing is done to explain the initial
cause of the trouble—namely Boris' desire (metaphysical
"angoisse"?) to forget about himself, even momentarily,
in the immediate sensation of pleasure—the guilt is repressed further; it transforms itself into the need to be
victimized.

The union is now complete. The victim needs to suffer
in order to expiate his feelings of interiorized guilt and the
sadists need a victim to satisfy their feelings of exteriorized
hostility. Thus, in the end, the various themes of the
book: duplicity, responsibility, reality, and repressed sexuality, explode with the shot which kills Boris. The parallel,
interconnecting, and chance encounters between people
and events which give the book its structure, as well as its
fluidity, all suddenly focus on Boris and transform suicide
into "murder." The events described in November, beginning with Edouard's sudden and improvised departure for
Saas-Fé, are climaxed by the dramatic scene in the school-
room where the reader realizes, in retrospect, that Boris
was playing Russian roulette with the six barrels loaded.
The six barrels are the seemingly fortuitous events in
Boris' life which precipitate his death.

Laura calls Edouard back to Paris because Vincent has
abandoned her. Edouard's relationships with Bernard and

Olivier prompt him to put Boris in the Pension Azaïs where the Puritan atmosphere intensifies Boris' guilt feelings. If only Sophroniska had not tampered with Boris' psyche, or had done so with greater skill. If Bernard, in turn, had been more solicitous. If La Pérouse had only committed suicide as he intended to and had not placed the loaded revolver back in the holster. If Profitendieu, instead of scaring the boys, had done something else. If, in the final analysis, the gang's sexuality as well as Boris' had not been repressed but recognized and, dare we say encouraged, Boris would not have died.

Boris' suicide, as Brée has pointed out, is the focal point of the novel. On the other hand, as Thody has observed, the theme of responsibility or irresponsibility links the story together. The varieties of counterfeit behavior falsify reality and set the stage for "murder." The social eagle Gide is attacking is the hypocrisy which leads to inauthenticity in others.

The sequel to *Les Faux-Monnayeurs* (1926), which was to be as long and complex a novel as the first, never fully materialized and was published as a "triptych" under the title *L'Ecole des femmes* (1930). Insomuch as Gide is now hunting family eagles or, more precisely, counterfeit elements in a husband-wife-daughter relationship, this book should have appeared logically after *La Symphonie pastorale* and before *Les Faux-Monnayeurs*. While the order of composition or publication does not really matter I suggest its place merely to situate the type of problem Gide is treating in relationship to the rest of his work.

Part I is written by the wife, Eveline, in diary form. Part II is a letter and is the alleged answer by the husband, Robert, to Gide's publication of the wife's diary. Part III, written by the daughter Geneviève, is an incomplete manuscript in novel form which she allegedly sends to Gide so that its publication will complement the statements of her parents. Gide has obviously structured a triple view of reality and has tried to give the reader a certain objectivity by stressing the exclusive subjectivity of each narrative portion of the whole. The novel is, among other things,

and, as the title might imply, a plea for the greater emancipation of women.

As for reality, Robert's "blind" espousal of social and
patriotic values gives him the same "sincere" hypocritical
attributes of the old despotic Azaïs. Eveline is closer to the
Pastor Vedel, since she is conscious of the false role she is
playing in pretending esteem for a husband she no longer
loves. Geneviève, though not an illegitimate daughter,
passes severe judgment on both parents and so, given her
lucidity and desire for authenticity and emancipation, she
might be compared to the illegitimate Bernard in *Les
Faux-Monnayeurs*.

In *L'Ecole des femmes* the dialogue of opposing values
is between the authoritarian outer-directed Robert and
Eveline, his wife, whose disenchantment with his early lie
about a journal each was to have written, but which *he*
never did, leads her to doubt and seriously challenge the
moral framework of his behavior. Gide presents a significant parallel between her inability to escape from the
mores regulating her existence, in spite of her insights into
"counterfeiting," and her daughter's determination to
strike a blow for women's rights. Eveline, while critical of
her father, her husband, and l'abbé Bredel (rhymes with
Vedel) submits to their advice, tears, imprecations, and
the sheer weight of circumstance, while Geneviève rebels,
makes sarcastic remarks about her father in her mother's
presence, rejects a stereotyped sense of daughterly grati-
tude for being alive, and openly criticizes her mother's
compromises with reality.

Robert unconsciously lives the lie of society's pretense
while Eveline is genuinely disturbed by the inauthenti-
city-of-being such pretense engenders. Ultimately, she is a
reluctant accomplice because the forces arrayed against
her leaving Robert are too great for her to cope with. Her
initial tragedy, of course, is that she fell in love with a man
she did not know better. She had the strength to oppose
her father and marry the man she loved, but she is like
certain women René Char describes in *Feuillets
d'Hypnos*. The surge of a large wave carries them over the

barrier rocks, but the crest is caught in a tidepool where, separated from the ocean, the once living water dries up and is transformed into crystals of salt.

Eveline's dilemma is that she is caught "high and dry" with a mediocre man who demands her submission and subservience. Her loss of self and identity is abetted not only by her husband, but by her father, the abbé Bredel and, we presume, by the rest of society. She laments her lot:

> So, the only thing left for me to do is to place myself in the service of someone whom I neither love nor esteem any more; a someone who will not be grateful at all for a sacrifice he is incapable of understanding and which he will not even notice; a someone whose mediocrity I was unaware of until it was too late. I am the wife of a puppet. That is my lot, my raison d'être, my goal; I have no other horizon on earth but this one (pp. 1288–89).[1]

Robert was to have been the glory of her existence. This idol shattered, she can no longer even believe in God. The abbé's advice that her renunciation will please God's eyes has a hollow ring for her since she will submit to circumstances not out of humility but out of pride. She has become a deliberate counterfeiter.

> All right! Since it looks as though I shall have to be satisfied with appearance, I shall assume a humble role, without any feeling in my heart of real humility (p. 1289).

She is all too human, however, and like Cocles, Damocles, and the men to whom Prometheus gave fire she sees purpose where there may only be gratuity. She interprets Robert's car accident as a warning from God to whose divine intervention she must now submit. We are reminded of Gide's description of the yellow canary in *Si le grain ne meurt* which landed on Gide's head as he was walking down the street. Little André was convinced, as he narrates the incident with the irony of an adult viewpoint, that this canary's particular flight somehow made him (Gide) divinely predestined.

As for Eveline's "humble role," Geneviève's commentary injects a typical Gidean irony:

> —What a beautiful novel I could write were you to dictate it! It would be called: *The Obligations of a Dutiful Mother* or *The Useless Sacrifice* (p. 1297).

Geneviève criticizes her mother for having made herself the slave of imaginary obligations. Damocles' eagle was his sense of obligation to an unknown benefactor. Eveline's eagle is her sense of duty to her husband, a duty which suppresses her own needs for the greater glory of her husband's mediocrity.

Robert's domineering attitude thrives at the expense of women who must remain submissive and subservient to men. He says, "Insubordination is always at fault. But in women I see it as particularly blameworthy" (p. 1322). The clash of values between Robert and Eveline is an extension of Gide's humanistic-authoritarian dialogue. Robert believes in the absolute need of an external morality imposed from the outside whereas Eveline, and in turn her daughter, believe in the ability of each individual to determine what is right and wrong. Robert's absolutism would deny this individualism on the grounds that it leads to trouble and eventually anarchy. Women particularly, he says, must be protected against pernicious ideas. He believes in moral censorship and the banning of books. In short, he defends his interests within the status quo. When Eveline tells him that, given their differences, they are not going to the same heaven, Robert reacts predictably enough:

> I protested that there could no more be two heavens than there were two Gods and that this mirage toward which she was directing herself, which she called *her heaven*, could only be *my hell*, hell itself (p. 1336).

According to him women need not worry about higher education because, in the first place, men should do their thinking for them and, in the second place, because women need only good manners. His daughter, of course, contradicts this attitude by saying that she had a "great appetite for knowledge" (p. 1383). Robert is the spokesman for most of the values which were anathema to Gide. Since Gide was challenging dogma in all its forms and manifestations (he is now attacking the myth of the infallible husband and male), he presents him as a counterfeit being who forces a hypocritical role on others. Like Azaïs, Gide sees Robert as the most dangerous "counterfeiter" because he considers himself sincere.

The unspoken premise of authoritarianism is that authority must exist because the individual is incapable of self-determination. If, on the contrary, we believe that man is capable of determining his life by regulating the choices he makes, then dogma is, in the final analysis, not only superfluous but evil. It is evil because, as Gide demonstrates in the effect the values of the Azaïs-Vedel clan have on the younger generation, it inhibits the growth of the individual, checks it, thwarts it, distorts it, and forces strange, devious, and circuitous behavioral patterns.

In describing his opposition to Eveline's argument for self-determination Robert echoes the authoritarian's classic criticism of humanistic ethics:

> while I continued to believe in divine truth exterior to man, revealed by the inspiration of God and transmitted under His watchful eye, she no longer admitted anything as true which she had not recognized as such herself, in spite of what I could tell her: that belief in one's own truth leads directly to individualism and opens the door to anarchy (p. 1325).

Robert defends the status quo. In Gide's eyes he is suffering from psittacism, the "disease" that so frequently infected Flaubert's characters. Robert, like Homais in *Madame Bovary*, gets ahead in life because he successfully mouths clichés and stereotyped formulas. There is irony in the fact that society would award Robert the "Croix de Guerre" as it awards Homais the Legion of Honor for "services" rendered. An additional irony is that the daughter's behavior proves Robert's point. Geneviève's individualism, in reaction to his conformity, does lead to anarchy because the stifled energy must expunge the force which is inhibiting it. What Robert does not understand, and what authoritarianism in general fails to comprehend, is that its restrictive quality leads to rebellion because, given the dynamics of growth and given the individual's need to fulfill himself, man, ultimately, has to discard all sheaths, wrappings, envelopes, and placentas which are not his own. Revolt, therefore, only confirms the notion in the despot's mind that greater restrictive measures are needed whereas, in fact, these same restrictions were the source of the trouble in the first place.

In *L'Ecole des femmes* Gide has amplified certain counterfeit relationships which might well have been included in *Les Faux-Monnayeurs*. Authoritarianism, in all its manifestations, is Gide's favorite target. His attack on it in *Les Faux-Monnayeurs* is less evident (though he in no sense spares old Azaïs or the pension) simply because there are so many other themes woven into the novel. The very linear quality of *L'Ecole des femmes*, which relates it to Gide's "récits," makes it possible for him, once again, to stress the "dialogue" of opposing values. Robert defends most of the values Gide hates while Eveline, though her behavior, in Gidean terms, leaves much to be desired, defends the values Gide himself approved of.

> Pretty soon [Eveline] admitted no Truth outside of man and no longer considered our souls [Robert is speaking] as receptacles to receive it, but as small divinities capable of creating it (p. 1334).

This is the familiar argument between Gide and his Catholic opponents. In fact, within *L'Ecole des femmes*, it is the abbé Bredel who tells Eveline that her "duty" is not to herself but to Robert. Robert, in turn, strengthens his position by allusions to God, the Church, and the abbé Bredel.

Gide's relentless irony undermines Robert's position. If Eveline must pretend love for Robert she will at least be honest with God. She refuses communion. Geneviève says that her father, in contrast to her mother, "placed a higher price on the appearance of virtue than on virtue itself" (p. 1352). Since Robert has no values of his own which have not previously been held by the in-group, Gide's irony, which also relates his work to Molière's play, from which it derives its title, is to have Robert paraphrase Molière on the virtues of keeping women ignorant. But in Molière "human nature" is forever triumphing against the forces (usually old fathers and even older husbands) which would thwart the youthful élan of daughters and potential wives.

L'Ecole des femmes, as a plea for women's rights, criticizes the male despot who draws his raison d'être from outside himself. Gide continues to undermine the tradition of the Church and society which stifles the growth of the individual.

The reader has, no doubt, noticed by now that the nature of our eagle has been transformed. Authority, as an interiorized voice which a character was either submitting to or is struggling to overcome, has been exteriorized and is now visible. Claudel, "big brother," Azaïs, and Robert are typical of a certain kind of man in a patriarchal society who capitalizes on fear, weakness, and hypocrisy in order to forge chains of moral conformity with which to bind mankind.

The invisible eagle, which Gide's early characters nurtured so assiduously, now appears in the heavens whence, those who would discern its flight, can, if they still think eagles beneficial, summon one to feed. Prometheus' eagle is, in effect, hovering over the Boulevard waiting for its meal. "Counterfeiters" feed public eagles on lies, theft, sadism, suicide, and murder. An eagle, therefore, is any force, internal or external, which frustrates the physical, moral, and intellectual growth of the individual. Authentic beings are not easy to cultivate. Those who know how, work against the counterfeit by exposing the nefarious effects of moral autocracy, religious authoritarianism, and family tyranny.

8

Saul, Oedipus, and God

On July 15, 1931, thirty-five years after Gide published *Saül*, he made the following notation in his *Journal*: "Upon rereading my play it seems to me to be one of the best things I have written, and perhaps the most surprising. It will be discovered some day and people will probably be astonished that it could have remained unknown for so long." That this play is one of the best things he wrote is perhaps doubtful, but on the other hand it may be as he says, the most surprising. Surprising, because this early work contains the familiar Gidean themes in a form so pure as to belie attention. Not until *Les Faux-Monnayeurs* will Gide be able again to combine such tension and complexity in one work. It is certainly true, as critics have already observed, that *Les Cahiers d'André Walter* contain all or most of Gide: the *cahier blanc* and the *cahier noir* are seen to represent the two antagonistic poles of his personality which will in turn create the "dialogue"; there is also the exaggeration of a personality trait which, like Alissa's asceticism, will lead the hero of the "cahiers" to madness and suicide; *André Walter* also contains the oblique point of view, the journal within the journal and a certain deliberate posturing, all typical of Gide's work. Though the reader may easily discern these basic Gidean elements, the work itself is tedious and dull. What makes *Saül* so interesting by contrast is that it too contains most of Gide but rendered in such a way as to become artistically viable.

The Saul-David narrative, at least as far as the external

details and action are concerned, is faithful to the Biblical version. Moreover, the Biblical drama of disobedience to God seems to have elicited harmonious vibrations in Gide's own revolt against transcendence. The dialogue between Saul and God (and even more, the absence of such dialogue) is Gide's further dramatization of the authoritarian and humanistic conscience.

The "surprising" aspect of *Saül* is not only that the polarization should exist within the same work, but that this play portrays Saul as an incipient homosexual. This preoccupation of Gide's, as yet unresolved, finds itself expressed artistically in the five acts of Saul's drama. In his conversation with the shadow of the dead prophet Samuel, Saul asks what his original mistake was and is promptly informed that he should never have welcomed David.

> "But since God had chosen him," says Saul.
> "Do you think," says Samuel, "that God, in order to punish you, had not already foreseen the latest vacillations of your soul? He has placed your enemies before the gate; they hold your punishment in their hands; behind your half-closed door, they are waiting; but they have been summoned now for a long time. You too feel in your heart these impatient expectations: you know very well that what you call fear is really desire." [1]

Samuel's statement is accurate enough since the person Saul both loves and fears is David himself.

Gide has insisted that each of his works is like the flowering of a rosebud, the bringing to fruition of inherent possibilities which are then discarded in the process of creation.

> How many buds we carry within us . . . which will blossom only in our books! . . . But if we wilfully snuff out all *but one*, how quickly it will develop and grow! . . . My recipe for creating a hero is very simple: take one of these buds, put it in a pot—all by itself—soon you will have a marvelous individual. Advice: choose preferably (if indeed you have a choice) the bud which bothers you the most. You can rid yourself of it in the process. [2]

Are we to assume that because Saul is a homosexual Gide tried to purge himself of this particular brand of sexuality? Since Gide did not reject uranism, we must perhaps conclude that either *Saül* is not a critical work, or that his theory has exceptions, or that his homosexuality was indeed a defect which he could never overcome (as he is alleged to have confided to a friend in later years). The fact that Gide's works frequently revolve around an "inner stain" (a defect of the personality acquired in childhood), explains his preoccupation with the uncommon and the sickly, as his botanical interest in the unusual species suggests.

In the Biblical version, Saul is rejected by God because he "feared the people, and obeyed their voice" instead of the Lord's (I Samuel, 15: 24). The fact that God prefers obedience to sacrificial offerings is echoed in Samuel's reproach to Saul, "to obey *is* better than sacrifice . . . for rebellion *is as* the sin of witchcraft" (I Samuel, 15: 22–23). It is useful to note that the *action* of Gide's play begins with Saul's order to kill the witches; but the witches he wants eliminated are none other than God's minor prophets. What is the meaning then of this juxta-position to the Biblical text which Gide knew so well and which seems to be the point of departure for his own play? I am led to believe that Saul, as he himself affirms, not only can no longer pray but that he is now in direct conflict with God, whose power to predict the future Saul wants for himself: "when I alone am capable of knowing the future, I believe I will be able to change it" (p. 16).

In Gide's play we hear Saul saying, "The philistines came: I was worried: I wanted to do the questioning myself; and since then, God has been silent" (p. 16). His initial disobedience soon metamorphoses into a desire to predict the future. Since to know the future is not a human attribute, his decision to appropriate this power from God by eliminating the prophet-witches suggests that Saul wants to be the equal of God, that he wants to be able to predict the future in order to influence it. Therefore, Saul adds arrogance to disobedience, and since pride is the greatest of sins (the cause of Lucifer's fall), it is not surprising to find Saul surrounded by devils. He is now doomed to suffer both the sin of his pride and the agony of his human limitations. The sin of pride is the ambition to fulfill all of man's potentialities, in opposition to God's omniscience.

The Bible is quite consistent in stressing the theme of obedience to God, and Saul, like Adam and Eve, has violated an order. Since God will not forgive him, Saul, in both the Bible and in Gide's version, has no recourse but to rely on himself. Moreover, Saul is an ambivalent creature whom Gide has created in his own early image; like Gide, he vacillates between his need to love God and his need to explore—having no alternative—the dimensions of his human potential. "I am perfectly willing to love God; —I used to love Him—but He has withdrawn from me—why?" (p. 61). The first devil answers: "To bring us closer together."

The emphasis in Gide's play shifts from disobedience and self-reliance to physical love, and moves frighteningly close to his own psychic conflict and private dilemma. The quagmire of *Paludes* has given way to an active struggle of opposing forces. As the incarnation of the humanistic conscience and the need for absolute self-affirmation, Saul is struggling for power with David, the representative of obedience to God and His imperatives.

Saul both loves and hates David. "Everything I find delicious is hostile to me. Delicious! my delicious one! would that I could be with him, a herdsman, beside the streams . . . my soul, which the song stirs ardently, would burn me less—leaping from my lips—toward you—Daoud —my delicious one" (pp. 105–6). Saul later clasps the devils to his breast under the royal tunic as he would no doubt like to clasp David. But as yet David is not only incorruptible, he is God's anointed son. Does he not consult and obey God's word in all matters and concerns? Is he not, in short, God's warrior since Saul is the leader of a thousand men while David is the leader of ten thousand?

Saul has not merely resigned himself to feeling rejected. He is willing to love God, but if God will not forgive (can pride be forgiven; and when indeed will Lucifer be saved; when will the marriage of heaven and hell take place?),[3] Saul, for his part, feels that he cannot repent. "Bah! it has been too long now since I have prayed. And even when I did pray, it was the same. The struggle will continue" (p. 86). Saul then is in active opposition to God and at times even seeks David's help. He asks David if he sometimes prays; David answers that he often does. Saul retorts that God never answers prayer, but David wonders, naïvely (a Gidean irony), what a king might ask that would not be granted.

> "And you," asks Saul. "What do you ask Him for?"
> "Never to become king," says David.
> "David! David! Do you want to join forces with me against God?" (p. 104).

To tempt David and, in Gidean terms, to corrupt him would indeed be a major victory against God. Saul soon realizes that this is not possible, and will try to kill David with his spear. But the ambivalence persists, and Saul will alternately (with Jonathan's intervention) forgive and pursue David. Symbolically, his attempt to kill David is a manifestation of his struggle with God—his wish to silence the authoritarian voice. But this act is basically impossible because, if Saul loves David, then to kill him would not only remove the source of temptation but at the same time destroy the object of his love.

Was not this also Gide's dilemma? If Saul, as a character, summarizes the temptations of revolt and of eroticism, and if David represents Gide's lingering fidelity to an ascetic Protestant morality, then Saul's death and David's triumph reflect a temporary resolution of the two tendencies in Gide's personal struggle. The very act of writing *Saül* suggests that the voice of God may still be strong in Gide's ear (1903). The play, therefore, dramatizes the two poles of conflict. Saul's death must be interpreted as the triumph of the authoritarian conscience so that *Saül* now

counterbalances the exuberance of the humanistic conscience in *Les Nourritures terrestres.*

The central theme of the play emerges as an attempt on
Gide's part to elude himself. If the play is indeed a
dramatization of a personal conflict, then Saul's attempt
to silence the voice of God at the same time that he is in
love with his anointed son David, becomes the quintes-
sence of Gide's personal drama. No wonder Gide finds
this early work surprising.

The oscillation between the two poles of his psyche
allows him not only to escape from the commitment of
choice; this oscillation also reveals his uncertainty, his
timidity, his alleged lack of self-confidence in groups or in
talks with Claudel. This duality, this uncertainty, persists
and is recorded artistically for our delectation and
glimpses of insight until it is resolved in *Les Faux-Monnayeurs*: "Does not the extraordinary difficulty I now have
in expressing myself also come from the fact that no imaginary characters inhabit me any more and that I strive to
speak in my own name only?" [4] Thus *Corydon, Si le grain
ne meurt,* and *Les Faux-Monnayeurs* climax Gide's
progression toward self-emancipation from the authoritarian conscience. His books are the record of this progression; the struggle between the two alternatives provides
the necessary tension for his creative genius. When the
tension is eliminated, as it was by 1925 or 1926, the true
creative spark dies.

Gide deliberately cultivated this tension on all levels:
creative, epistolary, and personal. He recognized how
strongly he needed it and how essential it was for his work.
Though the duality of this art was, for the most part,
spent by the time he published *Oedipe* (1930), it per-
sisted on a personal level in his *Journals,* in his relationship with Madeleine, and in his continuing dialogue with
his Catholic opponents. His trips to Africa and to Russia
and his "dialogue" with capitalism and then with communism suggest that the need for living in a climate of
opposing forces had shifted from the artistic to the social
level. In his earlier years the pendulum of his moral and

psychic evolution swings from *Saül to Les Nourritures terrestres* and from *L'Immoraliste* to *La Porte étroite*; from *Numquid et tu . . .* to *Corydon* and *Si le grain ne meurt*.

In spite of Gide's allegation that all his works coexisted in his mind and could have been written in any order, the alternating nature, the variety, and the stages of his emancipation from "authority" are more indicative than he would admit because, fundamentally, the struggle masks the dilemma of his sexuality: should he or should he not accept it? The voice of God says *no* while the voice of desire says *yes*. Gideans know that the great man fell in love with Marc (Michel in the *Journals*) and that in 1918 he went to England with him; that his wife burned his letters to her and that Gide returned to lament their loss. By this time he had accepted the duality of his nature even if others did not always understand it. Nothing seemed more natural to him than his spiritual fidelity to Madeleine, whatever his sexual *fugues* might be. Gide writes at considerable length of the devil and his temptations, for *le Malin*, as he calls him, up to 1918 possessed an uncanny and sometimes ambivalent reality. In this sense Saul's acceptance of the devils around him foreshadows the resolution of Gide's drama thirty years later.

Saul's failure, like the Prodigal's, is that he becomes a slave to desire, unable, like Michel, to rise above his passions. Lust atrophies his will and, while Gide approves of his rebellion against God's authority, he is critical of Saul's *total* submission to his eagle, desire.

Oedipe, published in 1930, answers many of the questions raised by *Saül* thirty-four years earlier. The key difference is that Saul's energy, in his attempt to affirm the human, is consumed in loving David and rebelling against God, whereas Oedipus' strength lies more in his affirmation of the human and less in his rebellion. *Oedipe* begins with an expression of serene pride in contrast to Saul's quizzical and almost plaintive dilemma:

I am Oedipus. Forty years old and for twenty years a king.
With my own strength I have pulled myself up to the
highest point of happiness. A waif and a foundling, without
citizenship or papers, I am glad above all that I owe
nothing to anyone but myself. Happiness was not given   to
me: I conquered it.[5]

Oedipus has no eagle of indebtedness (like Damocles')
and he believes only in the exclusive supremacy of man.
"It was I and I alone who understood that the only
password that would prevent the Sphinx from devouring
me was Man" (p. 283). Oedipus, at least in the beginning, feels that he alone creates his destiny and that this
élan toward self-fulfillment is the energy and very essence
of the gods.

Saul is in dialogue with an Old Testament God whereas
Oedipus' dialogue is primarily with Tiresias whom Gide
has created as a disguised spokesman for Catholic dogma.
Like Samuel denouncing Saul, Tiresias denounces Oedipus' pride. Nevertheless Oedipus' "punishment" is fundamentally different from Saul's. Saul's sexuality completely
erodes his being whereas Oedipus' grand failure has a
double explanation. He is the prey, first, of Jocasta's inces-
tuous love for him and, second, he is his own victim for
being blinded by a love which hides the secret of his
destiny. But Gide seems to place most of the blame on
Jocasta's initial deception since she married her son in
spite of the oracle's prophecy and the fact that she knew
who Oedipus was. Oedipus nevertheless blames himself
(and this is typically Gidean) for not searching farther
and for allowing himself to be enveloped in a total and
lethargic happiness.

What have you done, Oedipus? Dulled by my rewards
I have been asleep for twenty years. But now, at last, I hear
within me the new monster stirring. A great destiny awaits
me, lurking somewhere in the evening shadows. Oedipus,
the time for quietude has passed. Wake up from your
happiness (p. 289).

While Gide blames Jocasta and Oedipus blames himself they both resent that certain fatality over which their

actions have no control. Oedipus sorely laments the fact that his beautiful philosophy of life, with its emphasis on man, contains a flaw which brings him toppling down from the heights of his human achievement. He is angry at a predestination based on murder and describes the road of this fateful encounter, the day he killed his father Laius, as the "road of God."

While the two plays *Oedipe* and *Saül* begin and end differently, the dilemma each king has to face is that God no longer speaks to him. Each one wonders: can it be my fault? Saul tries to talk with God but He will not answer. Oedipus rebels against a God who would lead him fatalistically to murder. He wants no part of such a God and, therefore, instead of pursuing God's road (shades here of *La Porte étroite* and *Le Voyage d'Urien*) he sets out in search of man's road. Oedipus' change of heart explains why his answer to the Sphinx's riddle was so easy. He says, "What is there to look for in a God? Answers? I myself felt I was the answer to some as yet unknown question" (p. 288).

Oedipus was following God's road in order to find out whose son he was. His mistake, as he freely admits, was in abandoning the search. He builds his strength on an ignorance soon to be abetted and encouraged by Jocasta. Here is the initial flaw for which Oedipus is to blame, though Jocasta is no less culpable for her duplicity in the matter (shades here of *Les Faux-Monnayeurs*).

The meaning of Laius' murder is therefore ambivalent. On the one hand, it was preordained by God, and inevitable. On this level Oedipus is justified in resenting a fatality he does not understand and in whose hands he is a puppet. On the other hand Oedipus' revolt against authority (didn't Laius try to force him off the road?) is the seed of self-confidence which gives him such inordinate faith in himself, at God's expense. Oedipus has not only slain his father. His act would seem to be the symbolic negation of authority. Oedipus is in the same category as Gide's other bastards (Bernard, Lafcadio, and Theseus), since Oedipus was a foundling raised by foster parents, whose lack of family ties gives him special strengths and insights. We can therefore argue predestination as effectively as we can the "fatal flaw." Accordingly Oedipus' reactions vacillate between accusations of fatality against Jocasta and Tiresias and the searing blame of a self-inflicted punishment.

In the final analysis, Oedipus rejects a happiness based on error and ignorance. This is the occasion for a Catholic Tiresias to remind Oedipus of his sinful nature and of the power of God's redemption. Oedipus answers angrily that this crime was imposed on him by God before he was born: "the trap was set so that I might stumble into it. Because, either your oracle was lying, or saving myself was impossible" (p. 295). Tiresias alludes to original sin. Oedipus expostulates against a Jansenistic determinism and, finally, in his rage, blinds himself to atone for his error.

This ambivalent gesture, one of human pride as well as of atonement for past mistakes, is a refusal to submit to Tiresias or his God. Blind, Oedipus is now Tiresias' spiritual equal. Henceforth Oedipus will rely exclusively on his own inner vision. Nor is it anachronistic that he accepts to be led by the devoutly religious Antigone whom Gide has created as a Protestant of the Reformation. She tells Tiresias, the Church's representative,

> In escaping from you, Tiresias, I will remain faithful to God. It even seems to me that I shall serve Him better by following my father, than I did on your side. Until today I listened to your interpretation of God: but now, even more piously, I will listen to the voice only of my own heart and my own reason. Father, lay your hand on my shoulder. I will not flinch. You can depend on me. I will brush aside the brambles from your path. Tell me where you want to go (pp. 302–3).

Gide's delightfully ambiguous use of the word God and "father" establishes the same kind of reciprocity that worked so well in *Le Retour de l'enfant prodigue*. Oedipus' magnificent willingness to assume the burden of his own guilt, rather than bow down before Tiresias is, from Tiresias' point of view, the ultimate in pride. What it does, however, is reaffirm the absolutely *human* level on which Oedipus has been functioning even at the height of his agony and distress. Antigone describes this act of his as "the most noble" gesture possible, an act which determines her, the "joyless" Antigone never to leave her father in spite of her previous commitment to Tiresias and all *he* stands for. This is of course Gide's way of reaffirming the nobility of man. It is, in fact, a deification of the human to have a pious Antigone abandon Tiresias and return to her father with the words: "Tell me where you want to go." It is Antigone's words which make the ending of the play so trenchant since Oedipus says that he will only allow himself to be guided by her. Their union is now symbolically human and spiritual.

Saul's weakness contrasts with Oedipus' strength. Saul was devoured by a lustful eagle. In Gidean terms, had Oedipus submitted to the law of Tiresias' religion he would have acquired an eagle of remorse and original sin. Thus Oedipus is Gide's spokesman for the humanistic conscience while Tiresias speaks for the authoritarian. By sacrificing his eyes Oedipus overcomes the determinism of events, redeems his and Jocasta's error, expiates the evil he might have done (though not completely since his offspring will continue to suffer, even if this suffering is probably not relevant to the play Gide has constructed), and thus reaffirms the primacy of man. Saul's initial rebellion has been carried to a conclusion of which Gide approves.

9

Theseus

The publication of *Thésée* in 1946 was Gide's summing up of a long and distinguished career. Gide, however, is not Theseus. There are differences enough between them to make us look instead for Gide's character not only in Theseus but also in Aegeus, Daedalus, Icarus, Minos, and Oedipus. The Gidean personality encompasses them all.

Gide's notorious posturing, contradictions, his very "insincerity," represent his desire to capture and "manifest" the multifaceted complexity of life. This summing up of Gide's compels us to re-evaluate the linear simplicity of each work taken separately (except *Les Faux-Monnayeurs*, of course) and, instead, to look at the fragments as part of a coherent and logical whole. Theseus says:

> There is a time for conquest . . . and a time for purging the earth of its monsters; then a time for husbandry and the harvesting of well-cherished land; there is a time for liberating men from their fears, then a time to occupy their freedom, so that they may profit from their ease and make it bloom.[1]

Gide, like Theseus, also vanquishes monsters so that he may cultivate the garden of happiness. But Gide has interiorized the monsters Theseus slays or the Augean stables Hercules washes clean. For Gide the obstacles to man's "voyage" are not necessarily external, though he seems to have looked upon his dialogue with Claudel and his running feud with the authority of the Catholic church as Procrustean encounters. Claudel, Azaïs, and

Robert incarnate a "monstrous" morality Gide would pre-
fer to see eliminated. In his fiction Gide's characters generally wrestle with inner monsters, monsters of the imagination, duty, conscience, guilt, fear, passion, and even of
fatality. Prometheus kills his eagle, Oedipus answers the
Sphinx, and Theseus vanquishes the Minotaur.

Like these legendary heroes Gide has his own period of
monster and eagle killing. He destroys a diseased asceticism in himself by having André Walter commit suicide.
He rejects narcissism in *Le Traité du Narcisse*. *Le Voyage
d'Urien*, which leads the protagonist to the stagnant regions of a black Polar Sea, is an exposé of a soul's journey
in abnegation. *Paludes* is for Gide a purgation of hermetic
symbolism. The false prophet in *El Hadj* dies in his
attempt to lead his people into the salty wastes of the
desert. Michel, as we have seen, has an eagle, so do Saul,
Alissa, the prodigal son, Boris, and Robert.

Theseus, however, is one of the few Gidean characters
(like Lafcadio and Bernard, perhaps because they are all
bastards) who either does not have an eagle or manages to
survive it. He is, in theory (like Oedipus) born freer than
other people and can therefore use his energies to explore
his freedom rather than exhaust them (like Saul) in con-
quering it. It is not insignificant that Michel's parents are
both dead when he embarks on his "immoral" quest or
that Oedipus does not know who his parents are. Ordinar-
ily people are duty-bound by convention, social and religious mores, and/or the inner psychic stain of an emotional trauma. Gide, naturally, believes that most mortals
never conquer their freedom, not that they are incapable
of it, but that humanity has not evolved far enough to
make such conquest generally possible.

Gide's hunt for eagles and the slaying thereof was part
of his life's task even when the dialogue changed from an
aesthetic and religious orientation to a social and political
one.[2] Eagles, monsters, and minotaurs distort reality because they give man a false sense of urgency or of well-
being. Prometheus fed his eagle faithfully until he discovered that he was better off without it. In the labyrinth

Theseus is surprised that the Minotaur is so beautiful and he would have remained forever trapped by his lustful encounter with so handsome a beast had it not been for the string Daedalus gave him (not Ariadne in Gide's version). Like Saul, Gide might have remained trapped by his sexuality or his passion had it not been for the intellectual detachment, the link with himself which, like following the string out of the labyrinth, brings him back to a reality from which all other "real" encounters emanate.

It is significant that the labyrinth Gide's Daedalus creates is not one which holds its victims by force. Instead, the fragrance from certain plants and the smoke of fires drugs them into a state of euphoria from which they then refuse to be extricated. This lulling to sleep of man's critical detachment, like Homer's land of the Lotus Eaters, this symbolic labyrinth of man's in which Theseus gladly makes love to the monster who now has him in its thrall is a dilemma of many Gidean characters. Theseus escapes but Lady Griffith and Vincent do not. They are perhaps the purest examples of an egoistical sexuality which destroys them both: "even drunk, know how to remain master of yourself: everything depends on it," says Theseus as he recounts the experience of the labyrinth.

Gide seems to have practiced this advice diligently and, like Theseus returning to Ariadne, Gide, after his homosexual fugues, always returned to Madeleine and the reality of her world which was so different from his. But there is also an essential aesthetic dimension to inebriation and detachment. Gide maintained that his extreme identification with the personalities of his fiction was a kind of artistic delirium (not unlike the delirium of the Cretan labyrinth) from which, once the work was terminated, it was essential that he extricate himself by reaction. Hence the "dialogue" of opposites. "Art is born of constraint, lives by struggle, dies of freedom," says Gide in his essay entitled *L'Evolution du théâtre*.[3]

It would appear then that Gide cultivated and created as many realities in himself as he did in his fictional characters. Nevertheless, he seems to have believed in a reality capable of encompassing them all. His emphasis on being "disponible" was a warning to those who allowed themselves to remain enclosed too long within one mold. To view all of reality through the exclusive bias of only one of its facets was to deform the whole. Vision then, like Gide's *Thésée*, depends on our ability to grasp this multiplicity and weave it into coherence. Pasiphae, in describing her husband Minos and his family is essentially describing Gide's artistic ubiquity:

> He takes the view that, in order to pass judgment, one has to understand and he thinks that he will not be a good judge until he has experienced everything, either by himself or through his family. . . . His children, I myself, each one of us, in our diversity, are working, through our idiosyncrasies, for the advancement of his career (p. 1427).

Gide has in fact infused *Thésée* with his artistic polyvalence so that the thoughts, philosophy, and actions of the characters (not only Minos' and his family's) of his narrative correspond to variable dimensions in himself. Icarus is trapped in a metaphysical labyrinth yet, even though he is obviously not Gide, he speaks of man's search for the absolute in terms frequently Gidean. Icarus' limitation, unlike Gide's, is that his metaphysics, his only and obsessive reality, blinds him to the world and inhibits his communication with other men. Daedalus' labyrinth (or eagle) is his obsession with mathematical constructions symbolic of reason and intellect deprived of feeling.

> For me, these are enormous structures, palatial buildings heaped upon themselves with labyrinthine corridors and staircases . . . in which, as with my son's speculations, everything leads to a dead end or a mysterious "keep out" (p. 1433).

Oedipus tells Theseus that he has enclosed himself in a labyrinth of happiness based on a lie (a hybrid eagle).

While each one of these men has his weaknesses and his limitations each one speaks with a voice which, at varying times throughout his career, Gide also used. Theseus, for instance, gives credit to his father, Aegeus, for teaching him that nothing worthwhile in life is obtainable without a struggle. Theseus, like Bernard in *Les Faux-Monnayeurs*, lifts heavy rocks to develop his strength. This emphasis on effort is typically Gidean. Typical also is the "know thyself" advice Theseus gives his son Hippolytus. These words echo the waiter's comment in *Le Prométhée* apropos of the people on the Boulevard who are searching for their personalities. As far as Theseus and Gide are concerned this is a necessary activity since a preliminary period of monster-killing must precede the tilling of the garden of happiness. Monsters and eagles must be slaughtered before man can develop or enjoy his human potential.

Theseus, therefore, abandons a clinging Ariadne because she is an obstacle to his fulfillment. But Theseus also prefers Phaedra to whom Gide, with consistent wry humor, has given an identical twin brother. In abducting Phaedra Theseus has to disguise her as a boy, since Minos approves of a potential liaison between Theseus and the male twin. The knowledgeable reader senses Gide's comic play on his own deviant predilection.

Nevertheless, like Prometheus fattening his eagle in order to escape from prison, Theseus uses Ariadne in order to escape from the labyrinth. Analogously Gide, the artist, cultivates and feeds the many eagles of his multifaceted and Protean self in order to further his career (or escape his inner stain?). Theseus abandons Ariadne because, unlike Damocles, he refuses to be bound by a sense of obligation. He neatly rationalizes this exploit. Would Ariadne have been consoled by Bacchus and ultimately deified if he, Theseus, had not abandoned her? In the long run, says Theseus, Ariadne fared better than she would have, had she remained with him. If Madeleine is Ariadne, then her sojourn in heaven is perhaps a solace for Gide's heterosexual abandon. Nevertheless, if this is a Gidean irony, its implications of insincerity are indeed frightening. Daedalus says:

I have devised the following: to link you and Ariadne by a thread, the tangible sign of duty. This thread will allow

you, will indeed compel you, after you have been away, to
return to her. Be always determined not to break it, whatever the charms of the labyrinth may be, the call of the
unknown or the headlong urging of your courage. Come
back to her or all the rest, and the best with it, will be lost.
This thread will be your link with the past. Come back to
it. Come back to yourself. For nothing begins from nothing, and it is from your past and from what you are now
that all you will become must spring (p. 1433).

If the thread binding Theseus to Ariadne is symbolic of
Gide's bond to Madeleine and his early Protestantism, if
this thread is Gide's own sense of tangible duty which
always brought him back to her, even after his escapade in
England with Marc, then Madeleine seems to symbolize
the "best" in Gide, that very best which Daedalus reminded Theseus to come back to lest he lose all the rest.
Gide's lament, after Madeleine had burned his early letters
to her, that she had destroyed the "best," seems to corrobo-
rate this view.

The reasoned balance of *Les Nourritures* by *Les Nouvelles nourritures* and *L'Immoraliste* by *La Porte étroite*
reveals, I think, that while Gide was a sensualist viscerally,
he was a spiritual ascetic. The lean style, the classical
structure of his works, the telegraphic simplicity of his
dialogues which leave so much unsaid (and so much to be
inferred), are the reflection of a method deliberately conceived. It is a return to the origins of his Puritan self
which discards the superfluous and retains the vestments
of a pure nomadic "disponsibilité." It is this remarkable
fusion of a nomadic flight toward the sensual coupled
with a reasoned, though never prodigal return to puritanism which gives Gide's work its particular flavor and explains his Protean elusiveness, as well as the basis for his
"dialogue." Hence also, his insistence that every classicism
was no more than a vanquished romanticism. He is constantly shifting between the extremes of his visceral and
spiritual selves. His work is a study in such extremes. It is
an accurate, almost scientific, observation of the eagles
inhabiting the rarefied summits where misguided climbers
suffer all the torments of Prometheus feeding his eagle.

Thésée, on the contrary, is a study in serenity whose happiness Gide no doubt wishes his readers to believe was his. Yet Theseus' final and crowning encounter with Oedipus is probably Gide's answer to those critics who always insisted that Gide had never suffered. Theseus says:

> I am surprised that so little should have been said about this meeting of our destinies at Colonus, about this supreme confrontation at the crossroads of our two careers. I view it as the crown and summit of my glory. . . . Only in Oedipus did I recognize a nobility equal to my own. In my eyes, his misfortunes enhanced even more the greatness of his fall. No doubt I had triumphed everywhere and always; but on a level which, compared to his, seemed all too human and as though inferior. Oedipus had held his own with the Sphinx; had confronted the riddle of life with Man, the answer, and had dared oppose him to the gods. How then, and why, had he accepted his defeat? (pp. 1450–51).

Oedipus' defeat, his newly interiorized spiritual vision, now balances Theseus' orientation to the external world. Oedipus survived crises which Theseus never had to face. Yet both, in their affirmation—Theseus of the human and Oedipus of the superhuman—reveal how to avoid being pursued by eagles, gods, and monsters. Each king, in his own way, stands for an ultimate fulfillment by man.

Theseus' conquests were glorious but for all their glamor they remain earthbound, lacking the spiritual dimension of Oedipus' self-immolation. His unwillingness and determination not to submit to the gods and to destiny, his refusal to be vanquished by circumstance, is a heroic gesture which lifts him high above ordinary mortals. "I put out my eyes to punish them for having failed to see the evidence which, as people say, had been staring me in the face" (p. 1451).

Oedipus acts to preserve the integrity of human values. He is the most eloquent spokesman for the humanistic self who, even in his agony, and while recognizing the errors of his past, is determined to remedy them rather than fall prey to the authoritarian ethic of Tiresias. Oedipus' self-inflicted suffering expiates the error of his ways and disarms the vengeance of the gods:

> what I wanted to destroy was not so much my eyes, as the canvas they held before me; the décor within which I was struggling; the lie in which I no longer believed; and this in order to break through to reality (p. 1451).

Oedipus' reality is man's inner vision of the "divine," the human potential inherent in all men. Theseus' reality is to be found in the conquest of monsters (eagles) and in the cultivation of the garden of happiness. Gide effectively blends these two realities into his own final and serene vision of man.

In *Le Prométhée mal enchaîné* Gide criticized teleology and attacked progress. His final credo, while it by no means affirms the inevitability of progress, nevertheless maintains that man is capable of a greater degree of happiness than he has known in the past. In *Oedipe* Gide has Polynices and Antigone define the limits and preconditions of a happiness based on freedom:

POLYNICES   One cannot think freely without first smoothing the wrinkle which religious practices have creased the mind with.
ANTIGONE   Passions, the moment you give in to them, wrinkle and crease it more noticeably.[4]

Polynices and Antigone are restating the essential opposition between *L'Immoraliste* and *La Porte étroite*. Polynices is warning Antigone against the eagle of religious authoritarianism while she is warning him against the pitfalls which interfered with Michel's passionate quest for freedom.

The progress Gide believes in then, and he does believe in progress, is one of human perfectibility. He would slay the eagles of purpose and duty and replace them with a happiness engendered by man's creativity. Oedipus' answer to Creon's attack on illegitimacy appropriately sums up Gide's thought.

Certainly not—I don't at all mind knowing that I am a bastard. When I thought I was Polybius' son, I tried to ape his virtues. I kept asking myself: "What is there in me which was not first in my forefathers? Ever attentive to the lesson of the past, I looked only to yesterday for guidance and approval. Then, suddenly, the thread was broken. I had sprung from the unknown; no longer any past, no examples to follow, nothing to lean on; I had to create, invent, and discover everything: fatherland, ancestors. . . . No one to pattern myself after, except myself" (*Oedipe*, p. 272).

Gide's work, for all its variety, is a search for man's authentic being that lurks behind the façade of convention and the incrustations of stereotype. Gide's characters may be foolish or they may be heroic. Nevertheless their endeavors reveal a frantic need for happiness. But to be happy man must know what he wants. To know what he wants he must know who he is. Yet to know who or what we are is one of the most difficult tasks of all. The answer to the eternal riddle the Sphinx asks must, inevitably, as Oedipus answered it, be Man. Happiness then depends on man's ability to remain human in spite of all the forces that are continuously denaturing him. The fire Prometheus gave man has led him into the labyrinth of teleology. Man will emerge from its maze into the light of a new reality only after he has slain the eagles and the monsters that deform his human potential. Man's happiness on earth will be feathered with the plumage of eagles.

Notes

1 —Prometheus

1. Gide's version is entitled *Le Prométhée mal enchaîné* and was first published in *L'Hermitage* in 1899. Page references which appear within the text are from André Gide, *Romans, récits et soties* (Paris: Gallimard, Pléiade, 1958), pp. 301–41.

2. In commenting on *Le Prométhée mal enchaîné* Ramon Fernandez notes astutely that "the people who are horrified by the recent writings of Gide are scarcely frightened by this little book. Nevertheless, if I were they, I would consider it the richest in 'satanic' suggestions." (*André Gide*, Paris: Corrêa, 1931, p. 93.)

3. *Romans, récits et soties* (Paris: Gallimard, Pléiade, 1958), p. 291.

4. *St. François d'Assise* (Paris: Michael Lévy Frères, 1864), pp. 137–38.

5. *Man for Himself* (New York; Toronto: Rinehart and Company, 1947), pp. 143–44.

6. *Ibid.*, p. 158.

2 —The Symbolist Eagle

1. This and subsequent page indications within the text refer to *Romans, récits et soties* (Paris: Gallimard, Pléiade, 1958). *Le Traité du Narcisse, Le Voyage d'Urien,* and *Paludes,* the works discussed in this chapter, appear in the above Pléiade edition.

2. *The White Goddess* (New York: Vintage Books, 1958).

3. *Journal 1889–1939*, Pléiade, p. 40.

3—The Immoral Gate

1. This and subsequent page indications within the text refer to *Romans, récits et soties* (Paris: Gallimard, Pléiade, 1958). *L'Immoraliste* and *La Porte étroite* appear in this edition.

2. In his 1912 *Journal* Gide describes Switzerland as follows: "Here I am again in this land 'that God made to be horrible' (Montesquieu). The admiration of mountains is an invention of Protestantism. Strange confusion of brains incapable of art, between the lofty and the beautiful. Switzerland: an admirable reservoir of energy, one must go down how far? to find abandon and grace, idleness and voluptuousness, without which neither art nor wine is possible. If out of the tree the mountain makes a fir, it is easy to judge what it can do with man. Aesthetics and morality of conifers.

"The fir and the palm tree: those two extremes" (*Journal*, 27 January 1912).

3. In a letter Gide wrote to Claudel on June 18, 1909 from Cuverville he describes Alissa's dilemma in relation to Catholicism: "I can't imagine what can be *the* drama of Catholicism. It seems to me that there isn't one, that there couldn't and mustn't be one (unless one can say that it is all comprised in the Mass). Catholicism can and must bring peace and certitude, etc., to the soul: It is admirably devised to this end; it exists to *quieten* drama, not to *provoke* it—whereas Protestantism hazards the soul in adventures which may end in the way I described. Or in free-thinking. It is a school of heroism, the error of which emerges pretty clearly, I think, from my book. It lies precisely in that sort of superior self-infatuation, that exhilarating disregard of all reward (which you took offence at), that gratuitous reversion to the spirit of Corneille. But it can be accompanied by real nobility, and I shall have done enough if I persuade someone like you to pity and to love my Alissa—with a love that includes some small mingling of admiration.

"What I wanted to draw, quite simply, was the portrait of this womanly soul; a soul with which I fell in love for the same reasons that made you, also, pity and love her. A Protestant soul, in whom was enacted the essential drama of Protestantism—the drama which very few Protestants can glimpse, but which you described perfectly.

"This drama would not emerge in all its purity unless the element of external constraint were entirely removed. But I was afraid that, if all external motivation were discarded, it would seem paradoxical, the fear of buying her happiness at the cost of the happiness of somebody else—and, above all, the mother's 'crime,' and the resulting vague need of expiation and so forth. . . ." (*Paul Claudel et André Gide, Correspondance 1899–1926*. Notes and preface by Robert Mallet. Paris: Gallimard, 1949, pp. 103–4; *The Correspondence between Paul Claudel and André Gide*. Prefaced and translated by John Russell. Boston: Beacon Press, 1964, p. 92).

4 – The Pastoral Symphony

1. Jean Hytier, *André Gide* (New York: Anchor Books, 1962), p. 121.
2. *Journal 1889–1939*, Pléiade, p. 96. No date listed.
3. *Journal*, 30 May 1910.
4. See Francis Pruner's analysis of *La Symphonie pastorale* entitled "de la tragédie vécue à la tragédie écrite" (Paris: Minard, Archives des lettres modernes, no. 54, April 1964) in which the author effectively argues the close resemblance between the Pastor and the Gide of 1918 when Gide was writing the book.
5. 10 February 1912, *Journal 1889–1939*, Pléiade, p. 367.
6. André Gide, *Dostoïevsky* (Paris: Henri Jonquières et Cie, 1928), p. 59.
7. *Journal*, 3 July 1930.
8. *Journal*, 30 May 1910.

5 – The Protestant Eagle

1. Denis de Rougemont, *Comme Toi-même* (Paris: Albin Michel, 1961), p. 174.
2. *Les Temps Modernes*, March 1951.
3. André Gide, *Les Nourritures terrestres*. This and subsequent page indications within the text refer to *Romans, récits et soties* (Paris: Gallimard, Pléiade, 1958). *Les Nourritures terrestres* appears in this edition.
4. George Painter, *André Gide* (New York: Roy Publishers, 1951), p. 116.
5. Robert Mallet, *Paul Claudel et André Gide—Correspondance 1899–1926* (Paris: Gallimard, 1949), p. 240). *The Correspondence between Paul Claudel and André Gide.*

Prefaced and translated by John Russell. (Boston: Beacon Press, 1964), p. 225.

6. Justin O'Brien in *Portrait of André Gide* (New York: Knopf, 1953) and Catharine H. Savage in *André Gide: l'évolution de sa pensée religieuse* (Paris: Nizet, 1962) interpret *Numquid et tu . . . ?* as the reflection of a deep moral crisis which contrasts with Gide's thinking both before and after the 1916–18 period. I see it, on the contrary, as evolving naturally from what preceded it. I interpret the "crisis" primarily as an aesthetic stance more deliberate than involuntary. While each interpretation shades into its opposite it must be nuanced to do justice to Gide's complexity.

7. *Numquid et tu . . . ?*, p. 588. Published in *Journal 1889–1939* (Paris: Pléiade, 1948). Subsequent page references to this edition appear within the text.

8. See also André Gide, *Dostoïevsky* (Paris: Henri Jonquières et Cie, 1928), p. 178.

9. *Journal*, 5 March 1929. Subsequent date references from the *Journal* will appear within the text itself.

10. *Journal 1889–1939*, Pléiade, p. 555. This entry, without date, was probably written on or about April 22, 1916.

11. Ramon Fernandez concurs. He writes: "I must admit that I am absolutely unable to share the opinion of some critics who interpret *Numquid et tu* as Gide's giving in to his Christian destiny . . . when Gide stated to M. Martin-Chauffier that he felt *Numquid et tu* was 'more of a literary creation and relatively artificial,' I think he is much nearer the truth." (*André Gide*, Paris: Corrêa, 1931, p. 243.)

12. *Journal 1889–1939*, Pléiade, p. 777. No date listed. This is T. speaking, perhaps the initial of a fictional character whom Gide never developed. I see no difference, however, between what T. says and what Gide says.

13. *Journal 1889–1939*, Pléiade, p. 562. Exact date not listed.

14. *Journal 1889–1939*, Pléiade, p. 562. Exact date not listed.

15. *Journal 1939–1949* (Paris: Gallimard, Pléiade, 1954), p. 579.

16. *Les Nouvelles nourritures*, Pléiade, p. 297.

6–The Catholic Dialogue

1. "Personne n'a jamais parlé de responsabilité aussi souvent ni avec une irresponsabilité tellement prononcée qu'elle

en parassait maladive, irréductible. On demeure stupéfait en voyant comment, dans ses dernières pages, dans l'ultime même, il persiste dans son obsénité coutumière." (French translation from the Latin by J. Thomas d'Hoste; published in *Prétexte*, No. 2, November 1952, p. 8).

2. As quoted by Julian Green, *Diary 1928–1957* (New York: Harcourt Brace & World, 1964), p. 240.

3. *Ibid.*, p. 209.

4. "Feuillets," *Journal 1889–1939*, Pléiade, p. 1285. No date listed.

5. "Feuillets d'Automne," 1947, *Journal 1939–1949*, Pléiade, p. 309. Exact date not listed.

6. "Feuillets d'Automne," 1947, *Journal 1939–1949*, Pléiade, p. 310. Exact date not listed.

7. Charles Moeller, on the other hand, in his chapter on André Gide (*Littérature du XX*ᵉᵐᵉ *siècle et christianisme, I, Silence de Dieu*, 4th ed., Paris: Casterman, Tournai, 1954, p. 151), sees the "death of God" and the refusal of transcendence as the mortal sin of modern man.

8. Moeller (*Ibid.*, pp. 149 and 173) describes Gide as an irresponsible traitor. His work, says Moeller, reveals a progressive weakening of Gide's spiritual fiber and, in the final analysis, constitutes a religious and philosophical regression.

9. *Ainsi soit-il*, p. 1176. Published in *Journal 1939–1949* (Paris: Pléiade, 1954).

10. Moeller (*Ibid.*, pp. 162–63) accuses Gide of propagating a banal nineteenth-century "rational pantheism" and he (Moeller) dismisses Nietzsche and the "death of God" as terribly "old hat."

11. August 1893, *Journal 1889–1939*, Pléiade, p. 41. Exact date not listed.

12. "Feuillets," *Journal 1889–1939*, Pléiade, p. 776. No date listed.

13. *Si le grain ne meurt*, Pléiade, p. 550.

14. Jacques Lévy, *Journal et Correspondance* (Grenoble: Editions des Cahiers de l'Alpe, 1954).

15. Robert Mallet, *Francis Jammes et André Gide—Correspondance 1893–1938* (Paris: Gallimard, 1948), p. 300. Subsequent references within the text will be listed as Jammes-Gide Correspondence.

16. (Paris: Albin Michel, 1951), pp. 145–46.

17. *The Portable Blake* (New York: Viking, 1946), p. 667.

18. I must take issue with Catharine Savage's unequivocal thesis that during this period Gide was contemplating conversion. The Gide-Jammes-Claudel relationship is not all drama and turmoil. See Catharine H. Savage, *André Gide: L'Evolution de sa pensée religieuse* (Paris: Nizet, 1962), pp. 106-12.

19. *Journal 1889-1939*, Pléiade, p. 234. Exact date not listed.

20. As quoted in Jammes-Gide Correspondence, p. 352.

21. *Le Retour de l'enfant prodigue*, p. 476. Published in the Pléiade edition of *Romans, récits et soties* (Paris: Gallimard, 1958). Subsequent page references to this edition will appear within the text.

22. *André Gide's The Return of the Prodigal Son*, "Utah State University Press Monograph Series," Vol. VII, No. 4, Feb., 1960, p. 22.

23. "Feuillets," *Journal 1889-1939*, Pléiade, p. 676. No date listed.

24. "Feuillets," *Journal 1889-1939*, Pléiade, p. 342. No date listed.

25. It is only one step from "big brother" who speaks for the Father to the Prophets who speak for God. The role of the Prophets then will be to codify God's law as Moses did by bringing back the tablets of The Ten Commandments which were designed presumably to curb man's anarchic tendencies; but to make The Commandments stick, there must be an elaborate ritual, a system of rewards and punishments (heaven and hell, communion and penance) so that those speaking for the Father will be able to guide, control, and manipulate the behavior of the people they are trying to "civilize." The question of spiritual power and control then becomes one of singular importance since, without it, the centrifugal force of men's passions will tend to break away from the unifying edict of moral law. The more inhibiting the law the stricter the punitive and retributive measures, hence the wrath and vindictive nature of the Old Testament God. Sartre's Jupiter in *Les Mouches* affirms that men's remorse is a delectable odor for the nostrils of the gods.

Christ's revolutionary teaching was to proclaim that God was love and that forgiveness was virtue. Tolerance, walking the second mile, and turning the other cheek, though they may be interpreted as weakness can, on the contrary, be the foundation of a dynamic ethic for the transformation of man's hostility to man. Nonviolence as an active, creative force tends to be most effective when emanating from men who freely give of themselves, who are not coerced, and who evolve a program of action voluntarily. The history of nonviolence, including the self-sacrifice of the early Christian martyrs reveals, as Nietzsche has pointed out, and as Corneille's *Polyeucte* demonstrates, the unusual influence over others that such acts of self-control and self-immolation can provide.

While there have been and still are Catholic pacifists, historically, the two strongest and largest pacifist groups were the Mennonite and the Quaker sects—both Protestant. Protestant because there is this undeniable vein of nonviolence running through Christ's teachings which is, by edict, inaccessible to the Catholic masses. A significant element of the structure and emphasis of Catholicism is not on self-reliance and self-dependence but on obedience to the law as interpreted by "big brother."

26. "Etude Sur Auguste Comte," 1 August 1895.

27. The letter is quoted in the *Journal 1939–1949*, Pléiade, pp. 295–96.

28. *Journal 1889–1939*, Pléiade, p. 309. Exact date not listed.

29. Robert Mallet, *Paul Claudel et André Gide—Correspondance 1899–1926* (Paris: Gallimard, 1949), p. 184. Subsequent references within the text will be listed as Claudel-Gide Correspondence.

30. As quoted by Bradford Cook, *Jacques Rivière: A Life of the Spirit* (Oxford: Blackwell, 1958), p. 23.

31. As quoted by Blanche A. Price, *The Ideal Reader: Selected Essays by Jacques Rivière* (New York: Meridian Books, Inc., 1960), p. 47.

32. *Jacques Rivière et Paul Claudel: Correspondance 1907–1914* (Paris: Plon, 1926), p. 1

33. As quoted by Bradford Cook, *Jacques Rivière*, p. 78.

34. Jacques Rivière, "André Gide," *Chronique des Lettres Françaises*, January–February; May–June, 1926, p. 303.

35. Charles Du Bos, *Le Dialogue avec André Gide* (Paris: Corrêa, 1947), p. 301. Also Charles Du Bos, *Journal 1924–1925* (Paris: Corrêa, 1948), pp. 360–61.

36. 4 November 1949, *Diary 1928–1957* (New York: Harcourt Brace & World, 1964), p. 220.

37. *Journal 1889–1939*, Pléiade, p. 359. Exact date not listed.

38. *Les Caves du Vatican*, p. 864. Published in the Pléiade edition of *Romans, récits et soties* (Paris: Gallimard, 1958). Subsequent page references to this edition will appear within the text.

39. "Feuillets," *Journal 1889–1939*, Pléiade, p. 1293.

40. André Gide, *Dostoïevsky* (Paris: Henri Jonquières et Cie, 1928), p. 201. Subsequent page references to this edition will appear within the text.

41. Letter from Francis Jammes to André Gide, Orthez, 24 March 1914. Claudel-Gide Correspondence, pp. 227–28.

42. *Ibid.*, 27 March 1914, p. 229.

43. As quoted by Claude Mauriac, *Conversations avec André Gide* (Paris: Albin Michel, 1951), p. 40.

44. Charles Du Bos, *Journal*, Vol. IV (Paris: Corrêa, 1928), pp. 147–48. Subsequent page references to Volume IV will appear within the text.

45. *André Gide* (Paris: Gallimard, 1927), p. 127.

46. André Gide, *Et nunc manet in te*, p. 1134. Published in *Journal 1939–1949—Souvenirs* (Paris: Pléiade, 1954).

47. Gide to Du Bos, 10 April 1929. *Lettres de Charles Du Bos et réponses de André Gide* (Paris: Corrêa, 1950), pp. 178–79.

48. As quoted by Henri Massis in *D'André Gide à Marcel Proust* (Paris: Lardanchet, 1948), pp. 186–87. Subsequent page references to this edition will appear within the text.

49. See "Lettres d'André Gide à François Mauriac," *La Table Ronde*. January, 1953; *Gide-Péguy: Correspondance 1905–1912*, presented by Alfred Saffrey. Paris: Persan, 1958; Charles Du Bos. *Le Dialogue avec André Gide*. Paris: Corrêa, 1947; Henri Massis. *André Gide*. Lyon: Lardanchet, 1948; Henri Massis. "Le Mal ne compose pas. Lettres d'André Gide et Henri Massis," *Revue Universelle*. 1 (1938), pp. 100–4; Henri Massis. "La Confession d'André Gide," *Aspects de la France et du Monde*, 25 November 1947, p. 9; Henri Massis. "Le Drame d'André Gide," *Ecrits de Paris*. November 1947, pp. 76–83; S. A. Rhodes. "André Gide and His Catholic Critics," *The Sewanee Review*, XXXVIII (1930), pp. 484–90; Claude Mauriac. *Conversations with André Gide*. Trans. Michael Lebeck. New York: Braziller, 1965.

50. *Et nunc manet in te*, p. 1158.

51. "Feuillets," *Journal 1889–1939* (Pléiade), p. 1283.

52. End of September 1894. *Journal 1889–1939* (Pléiade), p. 50.

7—Counterfeiters

1. This and subsequent page indications within the text refer to *Romans, récits et soties* (Paris: Gallimard, Pléiade, 1958). *L'Ecole des femmes* is in this edition.

8—Saul, Oedipus, and God

1. *Saül*, p. 94. Published in the volume entitled *Théâtre* (Paris: Gallimard, 1942), pp. 1–151. Subsequent page references to this edition will appear within the text.

2. "Lettre à Scheffer." *Oeuvres complètes*, IV (Paris: Gallimard, 1932–39), p. 616.

3. See Gide's introduction to and translation of William Blake's *Le Mariage du ciel et de l'enfer* (Paris: Corti, 1965).

4. *Journal*, 2 May 1931.

5. *Oedipe*, p. 253. Published in the volume entitled *Théâtre* (Paris: Gallimard, 1942), pp. 248–305. Subsequent page references to this edition will appear within the text.

9—Theseus

1. André Gide, *Thésée*, p. 1448. Subsequent page indications, within the text itself, refer to *Romans, récits et soties* (Paris: Gallimard, Pléiade, 1958). *Thésée* appears in this edition.

2. Ultimately Stalinism was another eagle and Gide's dialogue with the spokesmen for communism in the U.S.S.R. in the 1930's was an attempt to slay one more monster devouring man and inhibiting his freedom.

3. A lecture first given in Brussels on March 25, 1904. Subsequently published in *Nouveaux Prétextes* (1911) and in *Prétextes* (Paris: Mercure de France, 1963), p. 148.

4. *Oedipe*, p. 273 (Paris: Gallimard, 1942).

Bibliography

WORKS OF ANDRÉ GIDE

In French:

Les Cahiers d'André Walter. Paris: Librairie de l'Art Indépendant, 1891.
Les Poésies d'André Walter. Paris: Ibid., 1891.
Le Traité du Narcisse. Paris: Ibid., 1891.
La Tentative amoureuse. Paris: Ibid., 1893.
Le Voyage d'Urien. Paris: Ibid., 1893.
Paludes. Paris: Ibid., 1895.
Les Nourritures terrestres. Paris: Mercure de France, 1897.
El Hadj. Paris: Mercure de France, 1899.
Le Prométhée mal enchaîné. Paris: Mercure de France, 1899.
Philoctète. Paris: Mercure de France, 1899.
Le Roi Candaule. Paris: La Revue Blanche, 1901.
L'Immoraliste. Paris: Mercure de France, 1902.
Prétextes. Paris: Mercure de France, 1903.
Saül. Paris: Mercure de France, 1903.
Le Retour de l'enfant prodigue. Paris: Vers et Prose, 1907.
La Porte étroite. Paris: Mercure de France, 1909.
Oscar Wilde. Paris: Mercure de France, 1910.
Isabelle. Paris: Gallimard, 1911.
Nouveaux Prétextes. Paris: Mercure de France, 1911.
Bethsabé. Paris: Bibliothèque de l'Occident, 1912.
Les Caves du Vatican. Paris: Gallimard, 1914.
Souvenirs de la Cour d'Assises. Paris: Gallimard, 1914.
La Symphonie pastorale. Paris: Gallimard, 1919.
Morceaux choisis. Paris: Gallimard, 1921.
Dostoïevsky. Paris: Plon-Nourrit, 1923.
Incidences. Paris: Gallimard, 1924.

Corydon. Paris: *Ibid.*, 1924.

Les Faux-Monnayeurs. Paris: Gallimard, 1926.

Journal des Faux-Monnayeurs. Paris: Gallimard, 1926.

Numquid et tu . . . ? Paris: Editions de la Pléiade, 1926.

Si le grain ne meurt . . . Paris: Gallimard, 1926.

Dindiki. Liège: Editions de la Lampe d'Aladdin, 1927.

Voyage au Congo. Paris: Gallimard, 1927.

Le Retour du Tchad. Paris: Gallimard, 1928.

Essai sur Montaigne. Paris: Editions de la Pléiade, 1929.

L'Ecole des femmes. Paris: Gallimard, 1929.

Robert. Paris: Gallimard, 1929.

Un Esprit non prévenu. Paris: Editions Kra, 1929.

L'Affaire Redureau. Paris: Gallimard, 1930.

Lettres. Liège: A la Lampe d'Aladdin, 1930.

La Sequestrée de Poitiers. Paris: Gallimard, 1930.

Divers. Paris: Gallimard, 1931.

Oedipe. Paris: Gallimard, 1931.

Oeuvres complètes. Paris: Gallimard, 15 vols., 1932–39.

Perséphone. Paris: Gallimard, 1934.

Les Nouvelles Nourritures. Paris: Gallimard, 1935.

Le Treizième Arbre. Mesures, No. 2, 1935.

Geneviève. Paris: Gallimard, 1936.

Retour de l'U.R.S.S. Paris: Gallimard, 1936.

Retouches à mon Retour de l'U.R.S.S. Paris: Gallimard, 1937.

Journal, 1889–1939. Paris: Gallimard, Editions de la Pléiade, 1939.

Découvrons Henri Michaux. Paris: Gallimard, 1941.

Morceaux choisis. Paris: Gallimard, 1941.

Théâtre. Paris: Gallimard, 1942.

Attendu que . . . Alger: Charlot, 1943.

Interviews imaginaires. New York: Pantheon Books, 1943.

Pages de Journal, 1939–1942. New York: Pantheon Books, 1944; Paris: Gallimard, 1946.

Robert ou l'Intérêt général. Alger: L'Arche, 1944–5.

L'Enseignement de Poussin. Paris: Le Divan, 1945.

Jeunesse. Neuchâtel: Ides et Calendes, 1945.

Deux Interviews imaginaires suivies de Feuillets. Alger: Charlot, 1946.

Le Retour. Neuchâtel: Ides et Calendes, 1946.

Thésée. Paris: Gallimard, 1946.

L'Arbitraire. Paris: Palimugre, 1947.

Poétique. Neuchâtel: Ides et Calendes, 1947.

Théâtre complet. Neuchâtel: Ides et Calendes, 8 vols., 1947–9.

Préfaces. Neuchâtel: Ides et Calendes, 1948.

Eloges. Ibid., 1948.

Correspondance Francis Jammes et André Gide, 1893–1938. Paris: Gallimard, 1948.

Rencontres. Neuchâtel: Ides et Calendes, 1948.

Anthologie de la poésie française. Paris: Editions de la Pléiade, 1949.

Feuillets d'Automne. Paris: Mercure de France, 1949.

Correspondance Paul Claudel et André Gide, 1899–1926. Paris: Gallimard, 1949.

Journal, 1942–1949. Paris: Gallimard, 1950.

Lettres de Charles Du Bos et réponses d'André Gide. Paris: Corrêa, 1950.

Littérature engagée. Edited by Yvonne Davet. Paris: Gallimard, 1950.

Et nunc manet in te. Neuchâtel: Ides et Calendes, 1951.

Ainsi soit-il ou Les Jeux sont faits. Paris: Gallimard, 1952.

Correspondance Rainer Maria Rilke et André Gide, 1909–1926. Edited by Renée Lang. Paris: Corrêa, 1952.

Lettres à un sculpteur (Simone Manye), preceded by a letter from Mme André Gide. Paris: Sautier, 1952.

Journal 1939–1949, Souvenirs. Paris: Gallimard, Editions de la Pléiade, 1954.

Correspondance André Gide et Paul Valéry, 1890–1942. Paris: Gallimard, 1955.

Romans, Récits et Soties. Edited by Yvonne Davet and Jean-Jacques Thierry. Paris: Gallimard, Editions de la Pléiade, 1958.

Correspondance André Gide et Charles Péguy, 1905–1912. Presented by Alfred Saffrey. Paris: Persan, 1958.

Correspondance André Gide et Marcel Jouhandeau. Paris: Marcel Sauter, 1958.

Correspondance André Gide et André Suarès, 1908–1920. Paris: Gallimard, 1963.

Correspondance André Gide-Arnold Bennett, 1911–1931. Genève: Droz; Paris: Minard, 1964.

WORKS OF ANDRÉ GIDE

In English:

Afterthoughts: A Sequel to "Back from the U.S.S.R." Trans. Dorothy Bussy. London: Secker and Warburg, 1937. Republished as *Afterthoughts on the U.S.S.R.* New York: Dial Press, 1938; London: Secker and Warburg, 1938.

Amyntas. Trans. Villiers David. London: Bodley Head, 1958, Dufour, 1961.

Autumn Leaves. Trans. Elsie Pell, with thirty-one other articles, including "Youth," "Goethe," "The Teaching of Poussin," New York: Philosophical Library, 1950; trans. Justin O'Brien in *The Journals of André Gide,* 1889–1949, IV, 275–81.

Bathsheba. In *My Theater.*

The Coiners. Trans. D. Bussy. London: Cassell, 1927; Cassell, Secker and Warburg, 1950.

Corydon. Trans. Hugh Gibb. New York: Farrar Straus, 1950; trans. Frank Beach. New York: Noonday Press, 1961.

Corydon: Four Socratic Dialogues. Trans. P. B. London: Secker and Warburg, 1952.

The Counterfeiters. Trans. D. Bussy. New York: Knopf, 1927, 1947. Republished with *Journal of "The Counterfeiters,"* trans. J. O'Brien. New York: Knopf, 1951.

The Correspondence of André Gide and Edmund Gosse, 1904–28. Edited by Linette F. Brugmans. New York: New York University Press, 1959; London: P. Owen, 1960.

The Correspondence between Paul Claudel and André Gide. Trans. John Russell. New York: Pantheon Books; London: Secker and Warburg, 1952; Boston: Beacon Press, 1964.

Correspondence between Gide and Valéry. *Self Portraits, Gide-Valéry Letters, 1890–1942.* Edited by Robert Mallet, abridged and trans. June Guicharnaud. Chicago: University of Chicago Press, 1966.

Dostoevsky. Trans. anon., intr. Arnold Bennett. London: J. M. Dent, 1925; New York: Knopf, 1926; London: Secker and Warburg, 1949; New York: New Directions, 1949. Reprinted with Bennet introduction and new introduction by Albert J. Guérard. New York: New Directions, 1961.

Et nunc manet in te. Trans. J. O'Brien with *Intimate Journal.* London: Secker and Warburg, 1952.

Extracts from the Journals, 1939–42. Trans. J. O'Brien in *The Journals of André Gide, 1889–1949.*

Fruits of the Earth. Trans. D. Bussy. New York: Knopf, 1949; London: Secker and Warburg, 1949.

Genevieve. In *The School for Wives.*

If It Die. . . . Trans. D. Bussy, limited ed. New York: Random House, 1935; London: Secker and Warburg, 1950; New York: Random House Modern Library, 1957; New York: Vintage Books, 1961.

Imaginary Interviews. Trans. Malcolm Cowley. New York: Knopf, 1944.

The Immoralist. Trans. D. Bussy. New York: Knopf, 1930, 1948; London: Cassell, 1930, 1953; New York: Vintage, 1954.

Isabelle. Trans. D. Bussy in *Two Symphonies.*

The Journals of André Gide, 1889–1949. Trans. J. O'Brien. New York: Knopf, 1947–51; London: Secker and Warburg, 1947–9, 4 vols.; entitled *Gide Journals.* New York: Vintage, 1956, 2 vols.

Journal of "The Counterfeiters." Trans. J. O'Brien, in *The Counterfeiters* and *Journal of "The Counterfeiters."* New York: Knopf, 1951.

King Candaules. In *My Theater.*

Lafcadio's Adventures. Trans. D. Bussy. New York: Knopf, 1927, 1943; London: Cassell, 1927; New York: Vintage, 1960.

The Living Thoughts of Montaigne (Essai sur Montaigne). Trans. D. Bussy. Toronto: Longmans Green, 1939; London: Cassell, 1939.

Logbook of "The Coiners." Trans. J. O'Brien, limited ed. London: Cassell, 1952.

Madeleine. Trans. J. O'Brien. New York: Knopf, 1952.

Marshlands. Trans. George D. Painter, in *Marshlands and Prometheus Misbound.* New York: New Directions, 1953; New York: McGraw-Hill, 1965.

Montaigne (Essai sur Montaigne). Trans. S. H. Guest and T. E. Blewitt. New York: Horace Liveright, 1929; London: Blackmore, 1929; New York: McGraw Hill, 1964.

My Theater. Trans. Jackson Matthews. New York: Knopf, 1952. Five plays and one essay (*Saul, Bathsheba, Philoctetes, King Candaules, Persephone,* and *The Evolution of the Theater*).

New Fruits of the Earth. Trans. D. Bussy, in *Fruits of the Earth*, pp. 181–293.

Notes on Chopin. Trans. Bernard Frechtman. New York: Philosophical Library, 1949.

Numquid et tu . . . ? Trans. J. O'Brien in *The Journals of André Gide*, 1889–1949, II, 169–87.

Oedipus. Trans. John Russell in *Oedipus and Theseus.* London: Secker and Warburg, 1950; in *Two Legends: Theseus and Oedipus.* New York: Knopf, 1950; New York: Vintage, 1958.

Oscar Wilde. Trans. Bernard Frechtman. London: Kimber, 1951.

The Pastoral Symphony. Trans. D. Bussy in *Two Symphonies.*

Persephone. Trans. Samuel Putnam, limited ed. New York: Gotham Book Mart, 1949; in *My Theater.*

Philoctetes. In *My Theater.*

Poussin. London: *The Arts*, No. 2, 1947.

Pretexts. Trans. Angelo P. Bertocci, Jeffrey J. Carre, J. O'Brien, Blanche A. Price. New York: Meridian Books, 1959; New York: Dell, 1964.

Prometheus Ill-Bound. Trans. Lilian Rothermere. London: Chatto and Windus, 1919.

Prometheus Misbound. In *Marshlands* and *Prometheus Misbound.*

Recollections of the Assize Court. Trans. Philip A. Wilkins. London: Hutchinson, 1941.

Return from the U.S.S.R. Trans. D. Bussy. New York: Knopf, 1937. London: Secker and Warburg, 1937.

Return of the Prodigal. Trans. D. Bussy. London: Secker and Warburg, 1953. Preceded by five other treatises and a play (*Saul*).

The Return of the Prodigal Son. Trans. D. Bussy. New York: Bantam Books, 1960. Trans. Aldyth Thain. Logan, Utah: Utah State University Press, Vol. VII, No. 4, 1960.

Robert. In *The School for Wives.*

Saul. In *My Theater*; in *Return of the Prodigal.*

The School for Wives. Trans. D. Bussy, with *Robert, Genevieve.* New York: Knopf, 1929, 1950; London: Cassell, 1929, 1953.

So Be It or *The Chips Are Down.* Trans. J. O'Brien. New York: Knopf, 1959; London: Chatto, 1959.

Strait Is the Gate. Trans. D. Bussy. New York: Knopf, 1924, 1943; London: Secker and Warburg, 1924, 1943; New York: Vintage, 1956.

Theseus. Trans. John Russell in *Horizon*, 1948; in *Theseus and Oedipus*; in *Two Legends: Theseus and Oedipus*.

The Thirteenth Tree. Trans. Robert Gottlieb in *Columbia Review* XXX (1951), 56–74.

Travels in the Congo. Trans. D. Bussy. New York: Knopf, 1929; London, 1930; New York: Modern Age, 1937; Berkeley: University of California Press (2nd ed.), 1962.

Two Legends: Theseus and Oedipus. Trans. John Russell. New York: Knopf, 1950; New York: Vintage, 1958.

Two Symphonies. Trans. D. Bussy. New York: Knopf, 1931, 1949; London: Cassell, 1931, 1949.

Urien's Travels. Trans. anon. New York: New Directions, 1952.

Urien's Voyage. Trans. and editor Wade Baskin. New York: Philosophical Library, 1964.

Vatican Cellars. Trans. D. Bussy. London: Cassell, 1953.

The Vatican Swindle. Trans. D. Bussy. New York: Knopf, 1925.

The White Notebook. Trans. Wade Baskin. New York: Philosophical Library, 1964.

SELECTED WORKS OF CRITICISM ON GIDE

Ames, Van Meter. *André Gide*. Norfolk, Conn.: New Directions, 1947.

Archambault, Paul *Humanité d'André Gide*. Paris: Bloud et Gay, 1946.

Brachfeld, Georges I. *André Gide and the Communist Temptation*. Geneva: Droz, 1959; Paris: Minard, 1959.

Brée, Germaine. *Gide*. New Brunswick, New Jersey: Rutgers University Press, 1963.

Davet, Yvonne. *Autour des Nourritures terrestres*. Paris: Gallimard, 1948.

Delay, Jean. *La Jeunesse d'André Gide*, 2 vols. Paris: Gallimard, 1956–7. (The Youth of André Gide. Translated and abridged by June Guicharnaud. Chicago and London: The University of Chicago Press, 1963.)

Fayer, H. M. *Gide, Freedom and Dostoïevsky*. Burlington, Vt.: Lane Press, 1946.

Fernandez, Ramon. *André Gide*. Paris: Corrêa, 1931.

Fowlie, Wallace. *André Gide, His Life and Art*. New York: Macmillan, 1965; London: Collier-Macmillan, 1965.

Guérard, Albert J. *André Gide*. Cambridge, Mass.: Harvard University Press, 1951.

Hytier, Jean. *André Gide*. Alger: Charlot, 1938. (*André Gide*. Trans. Richard Howard. Garden City, N.Y.: Doubleday, 1962.)

Ireland, G. W. *André Gide*. New York: Grove Press, 1963.

Lafille, Pierre. *André Gide, romancier*. Paris: Hachette, 1954.

Laidlaw, Norman G. *Elysian Encounter: Diderot and Gide*. Syracuse, New York: Syracuse University Press, 1963.

Lang, Renée. *André Gide et la pensée allemande*. Paris: Plon, 1949.

Mann, Klaus. *André Gide and the Crisis of Modern Thought*. New York: Creative Age Press, 1943.

March, Harold. *Gide and the Hound of Heaven*. New York: A. S. Barnes and Co., 1961.

Martin, Claude. *André Gide par lui-même*. Paris: Editions du Seuil, 1963.

Martin Du Gard, Roger. *Notes sur André Gide, 1913–1951*. Paris: Gallimard, 1951.

McLaren, James C. *The Theatre of André Gide*. Baltimore: The Johns Hopkins Press, 1943.

O'Brien, Justin. *Portrait of André Gide, A Critical Biography*. New York: Knopf, 1953.

Painter, George. *André Gide, A Critical and Biographical Study*. New York: Roy Publishers, 1951.

Peyre, Henri. "André Gide: Martyr and Hero of Sincerity," in *Literature and Sincerity*, pp. 276–306. New Haven and London: Yale University Press, 1963.

Pierre-Quint, Léon. *André Gide*. Paris: Stock, 1952.

Rossi, Vinio. *André Gide: The Evolution of an Aesthetic*. New Brunswick, New Jersey: Rutgers University Press, 1967.

Savage, Catharine H. *André Gide: l'évolution de sa pensée religieuse*. Paris: Nizet, 1962.

Schlumberger, Jean. *Madeleine et André Gide*. Paris: Gallimard, 1956.

Thierry, Jean-Jacques. *Gide*. Paris: Gallimard, 1962.

Index